WILD BEAUTY

BELLEZA SALVAJE

new and selected poems

Ntozake Shange

TRANSLATED BY
ALEJANDRO ÁLVAREZ NIEVES

SIMON & SCHUSTER PAPERBACKS
New York London Toronto Sydney New Delhi

Simon & Schuster Paperbacks
An Imprint of Simon & Schuster, Inc.
1230 Avenue of the Americas
New York, NY 10020

Please see Credits and Permissions on page 253 for information about the original publication of the previously published poems in this book.

First Simon & Schuster trade paperback edition May 2022

SIMON & SCHUSTER PAPERBACKS and colophon are trademarks of Simon & Schuster, Inc.

For information about special discounts for bulk purchases, please contact Simon & Schuster Special Sales at 1-866-506-1949 or business@simonandschuster.com.

The Simon & Schuster Speakers Bureau can bring authors to your live event. For more information, or to book an event, contact the Simon & Schuster Speakers Bureau at 1-866-248-3049 or visit our website at www.simonspeakers.com.

Interior design by Kris Tobiassen, Matchbook Digital

10 9 8 7 6 5 4 3 2 1

Library of Congress Cataloging-in-Publication Data is available.

ISBN 978-1-5011-6993-9
ISBN 978-1-5011-6994-6 (pbk)
ISBN 978-1-5011-6995-3 (ebook)

FOR LAURIE CARLOS,
a remarkable artist and a longtime honest friend
&
HARRIET SHANGE WATKINS,
my new granddaughter, whose life will
be that of a wondrous colored girl

CONTENTS

PREFACE

Poems come like a fresh breeze or a rapid slap to the cheek. The body vibrates, blows warm or chill, damp or dry, fingers tighten or relax and the lips grow thin or thick as the day I was born. Writing is so physical. Words pummel or caress.

The poems in this volume range from my early work in the 1970s when I could dance for hours and write poems till the wee hours of the night, when black-and-white movies of Dolores del Río or Bette Davis would keep me company. The music of Stevie Wonder, Benny Moré, or Cecil Taylor kept my feet in constant movement. The keys of the Underwood typewriter punctuate the clouds hovering by the base of the moon. So, it is mystical and of the actual moment that these poems come to you from my body and spirit. I wish I hadn't seen some of the life portrayed here; that the blood and tears were imaginary. Sometimes the myth and history of our people sustain me, regardless of the sweat, tears, calluses, and struggle we have endured.

I pull from the lush plains and jungles, deserts and snow-crested mountains and cement and barbwire of our landscape. We inhabit space with rhythm, color, and olfactory miracles. This is who we are. We are the colored people on the face of the earth. We must not let our oppression deny us the earth.

I want to leave something behind. An interpretation of our experience in this time with these people, this music, our leaps and pelvic gyration of all of our tribes, from Houston's Fifth Ward to Albuquerque. Someone in New York can levitate to the Mississippi or the Amazon with our ancestors of many different hues or our children with dazzling dreams. In love, giggling or reverent, ridden with tension or flailing with anger, we carry ourselves as if we knew something that was too secret for Anglos or whatever Other, we encounter. I bring this mélange of the lives of the colored people to you as I see and feel us, taste and spit out; what we have consumed, what we feed on.

Those of us in the New World, descendants of the African diaspora, survivors of the assault on Native peoples, *los guajiros del campo*, have never existed before. That is why we are the New World. We suffer from an ignorance of our tradition and language, our jewelry and crops, leading us to make ourselves up as we go along. Our languages, colonial, Creole, and colloquial, test boundaries imagined to be beyond our comprehension. We have outsmarted time and place.

Crack Annie, Rah Rah, the old Puerto Rican men playing dominos with their cigars remind us of our relatives. Hopefully, these characters bring us closer to a sense of self: honest and honored. Icons: Toussaint L'Ouverture to José Martí to lesser known heroes, Atahualpa and Denmark Vesey. We lace our visions with Celia Cruz and Aretha Franklin. Our suppers are shared with La Sonora Matancera, The Flamingos, Rubén Blades, Héctor Lavoe, Exile One, and Sparrow. We dance our sustenance in Bahia, Chicken Bone Beach, Roxbury and South Central L.A. We are everywhere. Just like slaves, we are in every country in this hemisphere. We are unavoidable, regardless of what they say. Here our voices and lyric are made clear. Our mothers' stretch marks, merely memories of our beginnings. Please come with me now and know our worlds, as I know them.

We can do it. We are remarkable.

N.S.

PRÓLOGO

Los poemas llegan como una brisa fresca o como una cachetada rápida. El cuerpo vibra, sopla aire caliente o helado, húmedo o seco, los dedos se contraen o se relajan y los labios se tornan más finos o más gruesos como el día en que nací. Escribir es tan físico. Las palabras golpean o acarician.

Los poemas de este volumen van desde mi obra temprana en la década del setenta, cuando podía bailar por horas y escribir poemas hasta las altas horas de la noche, cuando me hacían compañía las películas en blanco y negro de Dolores del Río o Bette Davis. La música de Stevie Wonder, Benny Moré o Cecil Taylor mantenían mis pies en constante movimiento. Las teclas de la máquina de escribir Underwood puntúan las nubes que flotan junto a la base de la luna. Así que, es desde lo místico y desde el momento real que estos poemas llegan a ustedes, desde mi cuerpo y mi espíritu. Ojalá y no hubiese visto partes de la vida representadas aquí; que la sangre y las lágrimas fuesen imaginarias. A veces el mito y la historia de nuestra gente me sostienen, a pesar del sudor, las lágrimas, las crueldades y las luchas que hemos sobrevivido.

Me nutro de las planicies y las junglas frondosas, de los desiertos y de las montañas coronadas de nieve y del cemento y el alambre de púas de nuestro paisaje. Habitamos el espacio con ritmo, color y milagros de una fábrica antigua. Esto es lo que somos. Somos la gente de color sobre la faz de la tierra. No podemos permitir que la opresión nos niegue la tierra.

Quiero dejar una huella. Una interpretación de nuestra experiencia en este tiempo con esta gente, esta música, nuestros saltos y giros pélvicos de todas nuestras tribus, desde el Fifth Ward de Houston hasta Alburquerque. Alguien en Nueva York puede levitar hasta el Misisipi o el Amazonas con nuestros ancestros de tantos matices distintos, o con nuestros niños y sus sueños sublimes. Enamorados, en la risa o en la irreverencia, colmados de tensión o agitados por la ira, nos conducimos como si supiéramos algo que es demasiado secreto para los anglos o cualquier Otro que nos encontremos. Les traigo esta mezcolanza de las vidas de las personas de color a ustedes, tal y como nos veo y nos siento, pruebo y escupo; lo que hemos consumido, lo que consumimos.

Aquellos de nosotros en el Nuevo Mundo, los descendientes de la diáspora africana, los sobrevivientes del asalto a nuestros pueblos nativos, los guajiros del campo, nunca hemos existido antes. Por esos es que somos el Nuevo Mundo. Sufrimos de una ignorancia de nuestra tradición y nuestra lengua, de nuestra joyería y nuestros cultivos, que ha llevado a que nos inventemos mientras avanzamos. Nuestras lenguas, coloniales, criollas y coloquiales, ponen a prueba los límites imaginados más allá de nuestra comprensión. Hemos superado en inteligencia al tiempo y al espacio.

Annie la del Crack, Ra Ra, los viejos puertorriqueños jugando dominó con sus cigarros nos recuerdan a nuestros familiares. Con suerte, estos personajes nos acercan a un sentido de ser: honesto y respetado. Los íconos: de Toussaint L'Overture a José Martí a héroes menos conocidos, Atahualpa y Denmark Vesey, enlazamos nuestras visiones con Celia Cruz y Aretha Franklin. Compartimos nuestras cenas con la Sonora Matancera, The Flamingos, Rubén Blades, Héctor Lavoe, Exile One y Sparrow. Bailamos nuestro sustento en Bahía, Chicken Bone Beach, Roxbury y South Central L.A. Estamos en todos lados. Tal y como los esclavos, estamos en cada país de este hemisferio. Somos ineludibles, a pesar de lo que digan. Aquí se hacen claras nuestras voces y nuestras letras. Las estrías de nuestras madres, apenas memorias de nuestros orígenes. Por favor, vengan conmigo ahora y conozcan nuestros mundos como los conozco yo.

Podemos hacerlo. Somos extraordinarios.

N.S.

BEAUTY IN WILDNESS AND WILDNESS IN BEAUTY

TRANSLATING NTOZAKE SHANGE

A sweet yet overwhelming challenge. Perhaps this is the most exact way for describing the experience of translating African American poet Ntozake Shange. Shange's poetry is not afraid of addressing topics that pertain to any black woman: political marginalization, the pain of racial discrimination, the contradictions these last two imply, physical and sexual abuse, the beauty in poor people, and musicality in a woman's love life. It's a matter of strong, fierce, colloquial, no-nonsense poetry; written for vulnerable and marginalized audiences, and yet playful, smart, cultured, wise. In a nutshell, Shange presents a mature poetic voice that comes from the gut in all its splendor, a verse that comes from the most intimate part of being a woman, a poetry that comes from an oral tradition passed down from generation to generation, as is the case of African poetry. If Maya Angelou can be considered the Martin Luther King of black poetry, then Ntozake Shange is the Malcom X of this genre.

Thus, perhaps the hardest part of re-creating Shange's poetry in Spanish is her informal spelling. This could respond to a way of showing class and racial difference in writing, which is key in the author's poetry. This feature also inserts Shange's poetry in the American Black poetry tradition with others such as Langston Hughes, Audre Lorde, James Baldwin, Maya Angelou, among many others. Informal spelling implies shortening words (*nothin, enuf, cuz, cept, walkin, comin*), fusing words (*haveta, sorta*), cultural references (to jazz, literature, and historical figures), generally not capitalizing words that normally would be, the lack of punctuation, and constantly using overlapping lines (phrases that begin in one line and end in another, thus markedly interrupting the syntax). While I've been able to re-create most format aspects, irregular capitalization, and most overlaps, in other instances I resorted to particular translation procedures. In "crack annie," I had to capitalize the names of the character "cadillac lee" in the Spanish version, because *lee* could also mean "to read," thus confusing the reader. Consequently, I also had to capitalize the names of the rest of the characters for consistency.

In order to make this translation work, the following translation procedures were implemented: compensation, explicitation, adaptation, and equivalence. First, the ampersand symbol (&) was kept throughout. Even though this symbol can be translated as *y* (and), I believe the ampersand is a visual element that can be preserved. The morphology was inevitably changed in Spanish in cases in which the poetic voice speaks clearly to a woman or as a woman yet using gender-neutral words—*child, kid,* or *friend,* as in "poemas para una amiga" ("poem for a friend"). Furthermore, close attention was paid to matters of class and race, as well as cultural references. In this sense, I chose the Afro-Latino Caribbean as a space for placing Shange's work because this region has a well-established, rich,

Black poetry tradition. Authors like Nicolás Guillén and Nancy Morejón (Cuba), Manuel del Cabral (Dominican Republic), as well as Luis Palés Matos and Fortunato Vizcarrondo (Puerto Rico)—who I grew up with as a reader—among others, provide a solid reference for a Spanish version of Ntozake Shange's work. Most translation decisions in this text originate from this cultural space.

Nevertheless, perhaps the hardest part was reproducing an informal spelling in Spanish comparable to Shange's. Her poetry shows an English spelling that responds to orality: she writes as English sounds phonetically. The problem is that this is the very same norm in which Spanish works—spelling in our language directly responds to the way in which the words are pronounced. Thus, it was impossible to reproduce the exact instances in which words were modified. I have taken advantage of the words ending in -ada or -ado, or in -dad, and shortened them to –á, -ao, or -dá. This is the case of separá, enojao, realidá, among others. The same principle was applied to nada and para, which were rendered as ná and pa; the case of forms todo, todos, toda, todos modified to tó, tós, toa, toas, is similar (the accent in the masculine forms avoids confusion with tos (cough). These abbreviations are very common in spoken Spanish. In the same way, I fused words in order to replicate the author's style because the distinction would not be made in spoken Spanish. This is the case of estabaquí, delos, dela, deque . . . among others. A particular case is sufisiente because it seems to me that enuf is too much an important word in the author's work, thus requiring a visual mark in Spanish to highlight its spelling. In addition, the s opens the door for a play in meaning allowed by Shange's spelling.

Terms referring to skin tone in a racial context were also a problem. It seems to me that the author uses the pejorative word *niggah* in order to show a political, historical, and social context that weighs in such a controversial word. In order to re-create this semantic load, I propose *maldita negra* or *jodía negra*, because it is an effective way of rendering such a negative word. In the case of *red niggah*, the author has made it clear that this term points to a skin tone that is not too dark nor too light, a mixed skin tone, a word used in the Midwest and the South—where Shange grew up—to refer to Native Americans, hence the *red*. Shange suggested using *india negrita*, and I have respected her criterion in this matter.

In the case of people of lighter, yet not white, skin, there is a reference to the color yellow—*yellah girl*. I used the term *jabá* (masculine, *jabao*), used in the Afro-Latino Caribbean to refer to people of white or light skin color with physical features—nose, cheeks, hair, thighs, etc.—related to black people. Regarding *brown*, a skin tone in between black and white, I used *trigueña* and *morena*. The first term is a euphemism for a mixed-race skin tone—literally, the color of wheat—yet in truth, this term is used for referring to darker skin tones. The same situation pertains to *morena*, which points to mixed-race skin, but is commonly used as a euphemism for dark skin tones. These two terms work very well in the Hispanic Caribbean when referring to mixed skin tones, which are implied in English by the term *brown*.

Adaptation, equivalence, and explicitation were used to translate cultural references. *Papa Legbé* was translated by the equivalent term for this Yoruba deity in Spanish, *Eleguá*, more identifiable in the Afro-Latino world. Similarly, references to children's stories of *rose red* and *rose white* were adapted as *cenicienta* (Cinderella) and *blanca nieves* (Snow White), because they are universally known throughout the Spanish-speaking world. Song lyrics used by the author in poems were translated as best as possible, except in cases in which she asked to keep specific lines in English. In the Spanish version of "take the A train," I used explicitation when translating a wordplay on the famous line by Mick Jagger and Keith Richards, "(I Can't Get No) Satisfaction," recorded by Otis Redding, a necessary addition so that the reader can identify the song without any doubt. In the Spanish version of "Shortnin' Bread," I had to adapt the entire lines pertaining to a children's rhyme intended for little black girls with a stanza from the poem "Duerme negrito" by Nicolás Guillén. The poem itself is a black version of an Atahualpa Yupanqui song, and thus, it is a well-known reference in the Spanish-speaking world. I then used the popular song "La pelusa" to recreate a rhyme in which a white girl is invited to dance.

There were other minor modifications that I can't include due to lack of space, yet I want to mention the use of *peso* and *moneda* for *dime*. The first was used to indicate a coin of low value that would be universally known throughout Latin America. The second was used as an option for *coin* due to a lack of a colloquial word in Spanish that would be valid for all Spanish speakers.

The end product is a Spanish text that renders the colloquial nature, the playful and desolating tone, the musical and poetic register of Ntozake Shange. Her poetry in Spanish can be situated in the tradition of Black poetry that can be seen in recent Afro-Caribbean authors, like Puerto Rico's Anjelamaría Dávila. The poems are well-written, strong, overwhelming, and it is also a poetry disconnected from the formalities of the poetic world. In Ntozake Shange I've had the privilege of finding a mentor in all the senses of the word, because her poetry comprehends all roles—from how much poetry can hurt to how high a poem can fly. It has been a wild adventure, filled with beauty.

ALEJANDRO ÁLVAREZ NIEVES, PhD
San Juan, Puerto Rico

BELLEZA EN LO SALVAJE Y SALVAJISMO EN LO BELLO

TRADUCIR A NTOZAKE SHANGE

Un reto arrollador y dulce a la vez. Quizás esta sea la forma
más precisa de describir la experiencia de traducir a la poeta
afroestadounidense Ntozake Shange. Estamos ante una poesía
que no escatima en abordar temas que conciernen a toda mujer
negra: la marginalidad política, el dolor de la discriminación
racial, las contradicciones que estas dos suponen, lo bello en
la pobreza de la gente, la musicalidad de la vida íntima de
una mujer. Es una poesía dura, feroz, sin tapujos, coloquial,
dirigida a públicos vulnerables y marginados, pero a la vez
lúdica, astuta, culta, sabia. En fin, Shange nos presenta en todo
su esplendor una voz madura que proviene del vientre, de lo
más íntimo de la mujer desde una tradición oral que pasa de
generación en generación, como suele ser la poesía de origen
africano. Si se puede decir que Maya Angelou es la Martin
Luther King de la poesía afrodescendiente, entonces Ntozake
Shange es la Malcom X de este género literario.

Así, quizás el rasgo de la poesía de esta autora más difí-
cil de recrear en español es su informalidad en la grafía del
inglés. Entendemos que esto responde a una forma particular

de demostrar en la escritura una diferencia de clase y raza que es clave en la poesía de la autora. Asimismo, es una forma de incorporarse en la tradición de la poesía negra estadounidense, con Langston Hughes, Audre Lorde, James Baldwin, Maya Angelou, entre muchos otros. La escritura informal de Shange supone el acortamiento de palabras (*nothin, enuf, cuz, cept, walkin, comin*), la unión de palabras (*haveta, sorta*), referencias culturales (al mundo del jazz, la literatura y la historia), el uso de la minúscula en casi todo momento, la falta de signos de puntuación y el uso frecuente del encabalgamiento (frases que comienzan en un verso y acaban en otro en una interrupción sintáctica marcada). Si bien hemos podido recrear los aspectos de formato, la minúscula preponderante y la mayoría de los encabalgamientos, en otras ocasiones hemos recurrido a procedimientos de traducción particulares. En el caso específico del poema "crack annie", tuve que usar la mayúscula inicial en el nombre del personaje *cadillac lee* para evitar la confusión con el verbo *leer*. Por consiguiente, usé la mayúscula inicial para el personaje *berneatha* y para el resto de las personas mencionadas por cuestiones de uniformidad.

Para lograr esta traducción, destacamos el uso de los siguientes procedimientos de traducción: la compensación, la explicitación, la adaptación y la equivalencia. En primer lugar, hemos mantenido el símbolo *et* latino (*ampersand* en inglés): &. Aunque se puede traducir por *y*, nos parece un elemento visual de la autora que se puede conservar. Hemos cambiado la morfología, inevitablemente, al género femenino en los casos en que la voz poética se dirige claramente a una mujer pero que usa palabras sin género marcado, como *child, kid* o *friend*, como en el poema "palabras para una amiga". Más aun, hemos prestado mucha atención a las cuestiones de raza y clase, así como a las referencias culturales. En este caso, hemos escogido el Caribe afrolatino como espacio para ubicar la poesía de Shange, porque tiene una tradición de poesía negra rica y muy establecida. Autores como Nicolás Guillén y Nancy Morejón (Cuba), Manuel del Cabral (República Dominicana), así como Luis Palés Matos y Fortunato Vizcarrondo (Puerto Rico) —con los que me crie como lector—, entre otros, nos dan un referente para una versión en español de Ntozake Shange. Es desde este espacio cultural afrolatino donde parten la mayoría de las decisiones de traducción de este texto.

Dicho esto, quizás lo más difícil fue reproducir una grafía informal en español comparable con la de Shange. Y es que su poesía presenta una grafía del inglés que responde a su oralidad: escribe un inglés que responde a la fonética. El problema es que esa misma es la norma bajo la cual funciona el español: la ortografía de nuestra lengua responde directamente a cómo se pronuncian las palabras. Así, no ha sido posible reproducir las instancias exactas en las que se modifican palabras, pero sí hemos podido compensar esta particularidad con otras. Hemos aprovechado las palabras que terminan en *-ada* y *-ado*, así como las que terminan en *-dad*, y las hemos modificado para que terminen en *-á*, *-ao* o *-dá*. Es el caso de palabras como *separá*, *enojao*, *realidá*, entre otras. Siguiendo este principio, hemos modificado *nada* y *para* a *ná* y *pa*; lo mismo con las formas *todo*, *toda*, *todos*, *todas*, que se modificaron a *tó*, *toa*, *tós*, *toas* (el acento del masculino es para no confundirla con *tos* de *toser*). Estas abreviaciones coloquiales son muy comunes en la lengua hablada del español. Asimismo, hemos fusionado palabras para replicar esa particularidad de la autora, pues en la lengua hablada no se distinguirían. Es el caso de *estabaquí, delos, dela, deque* . . . entre otros. Un caso particular es el de *sufisiente*, pues nos parece que *enuf* es una palabra importantísima para la poesía de la autora, y requiere de una marca visual que la distinga en español. Además, abre la puerta a un juego de significados que entendemos está permitido por la ortografía de la autora.

Los términos que refieren al tono del color de la piel, en un contexto racial, también presentaron sus dificultades. Nos parece que la autora utiliza el peyorativo *niggah* para fines de demostrar el contexto político-social e histórico que pesa en esa palabra tan polémica. Para reproducirlo, hemos propuesto *maldita negra* y *jodía negra*, pues nos parece que es lo que recoge esa carga tan negativa. En el caso de *red niggah*, la autora nos aclaró que el término apunta a una tonalidad de piel que no es muy clara ni muy oscura, una piel mestiza, que en el medio oeste y sur de Estados Unidos, donde se crio Shange, se identificaba con los indígenas; de ahí lo de rojo. La autora nos recomendó *india negrita* para este caso, y hemos respetado su criterio. En el caso de las personas de color cuya tez es clara, pero no blanca, notamos la referencia al amarillo (*yellah girl*). En este caso, preferimos el término *jabá* (masculino, *jabao*), que se usa en el Caribe afrolatino para las personas blancas o de tez bien clara que tienen rasgos físicos atribuidos a los de raza negra (nariz, pómulos, pelo, caderas, etc.). En cuanto a *brown*, un tono de piel mestiza entre el blanco y el negro, hemos utilizado *trigueña* y *morena*. El primer término es un eufemismo para las personas de piel mestiza (color del trigo), pero que en realidad apunta en muchos casos a un tono de piel más oscuro. Lo mismo pasa con el segundo, que apunta a la piel mestiza, pero es un eufemismo para la piel más oscura. Ambos funcionan muy bien en el Caribe afrolatino para hablar de la piel de tonos híbridos, que en inglés se recoge en el término *brown*.

La adaptación, la equivalencia y la explicitación se usaron en las referencias culturales. Para *Papa Legbé*, preferimos llamar al orisha yoruba con el equivalente *Eleguá*, más identificable en el mundo hispano. De la misma manera, las referencias a cuentos infantiles de *rose red* y *rose white* se adaptaron a *cenicienta* y *blanca nieves*, de referencia universal en el mundo de habla hispana. Las letras de canciones que la autora usa en sus poemas se tradujeron lo mejor posible, salvo en los casos en que ella misma ha pedido dejarlas en inglés. En la versión en español de "take the A train", hice uso de la explicitación al traducir el juego de palabras con el famoso verso de Mick Jagger y Keith Richards, "(I Can't Get No) Satisfaction", grabado por Otis Redding, una adición necesaria para que el lector pueda identificar la referencia sin dudas. En el poema "la bebé de mamá", hubo que adaptar la rima infantil que apunta a una canción para niñas negras al poema "Duerme negrito" de Nicolás Guillén, a su vez una versión de una nana atribuida a Atahualpa Yupanqui, y, por ende, de mucho arraigo en Latinoamérica. También hemos recurrido a una canción muy popular, "La pelusa", que cuenta con varias adaptaciones, para buscar una estrofa en la que se invita a una niña blanca a bailar.

Hubo otras modificaciones menores que no podemos añadir por falta de espacio, salvo algunas cosas que quisiera destacar. La primera es el uso de *peso* y *moneda* como equivalentes de *dime*. El primero es porque es un término muy conocido como moneda de poco valor, y la segunda es una modulación a falta de un término coloquial para moneda de diez centavos que sea reconocido universalmente en el mundo del español.

Al final, hemos logrado un texto que recoge el tono coloquial, lúdico y desgarrador, la musicalidad y el registro poético de Ntozake Shange. Su poesía en español se ubica en la tradición de la poesía negra que se ve en autoras afrocaribeñas recientes, como la puertorriqueña Anjelamaría Dávila. Es una poesía de altura, fuerte, imponente, pero a la vez desvinculada de las formalidades del mundo (y del mundillo) poético. En Ntozake Shange he tenido el privilegio de encontrar una mentora en todos los sentidos, porque su poesía abarca todos los ámbitos: desde lo que puede doler la poesía hasta dónde puede elevarse el verbo. Ha sido una aventura salvaje, llena de belleza.

ALEJANDRO ÁLVAREZ NIEVES, PHD
San Juan, Puerto Rico

WILD
BEAUTY

BELLEZA
SALVAJE

necesitamos un dios que sangre ahora

necesitamos un dios que sangre ahora
un dios cuyas heridas no sean
una pequeña venganza macho
una concesión lamentable a la humildad
un desierto arrasado con secarse al tuétano en honor al señor

necesitamos un dios que sangre
que extienda su vulva lunar & nos bañe de sombras escarlata
gruesa y caliente como el aliento de sus
propias madres que se desgarran   pa dejarnos   entrar
este lugar se abre de par en par
así como nuestras madres sangran
el planeta puja   de luto por nuestra ignorancia
la luna tira de los mares
pa que la sostengan/ pa que la sostengan
abracen las colinas hinchadas/ no estoy
herida me desangro a la vida

necesitamos un dios que sangre ahora
cuyas heridas no sean el fin de ná

we need a god who bleeds now

we need a god who bleeds now
a god whose wounds are not
some small male vengeance
some pitiful concession to humility
a desert swept with dryin marrow in honor of the lord

we need a god who bleeds
spreads her lunar vulva & showers us in shades of scarlet
thick & warm like the breath of her
our mothers tearing   to let us   in
this place breaks open
like our mothers bleeding
the planet is heaving   mourning our ignorance
the moon tugs the seas
to hold her/ to hold her
embrace swelling hills/ i am
not wounded i am bleeding to life

we need a god who bleeds now
whose wounds are not the end of anything

From *a daughter's geography*

del quimbombó a las verduras

tengo que bajarle el volumen a mi tele aveces porque
no soporto que la gente blanca/ me grite/
aveces la apago
pues no puedo verlos enmi cuarto tampoco/
así tan blancos
por eso me gustan/ las verduras/
no pueden ni olerte/ no sabrían cuál es tu sabor
sin escabullirse/ no tienen
idea de que deberían recibir el hormigueo del picante & un baño de
     vinagre
licores caseros esparcidos sobre rollos calientes

tengo que apagar la tele porque la gente blanca
sigue jugando juegos/ & sigue presidentes que vacacionan en la guerra
hay un problema grave de olores en la tele también/que
me regresa a las verduras

recuerdo a agüela en el mercado eligiendo nabos
berzas y hojas de mostaza/ pa mezclarlas/ echa ½ moña magra
ahí con un poco de pernil & ay dios qué rico/
viví con ella en su cocina/ con las verduras que podía conseguir
sí la mera raíz de mí misma
          la tierra & los bichitos que buscaba en las coles frescas/
          despejando cada hoja bien lento/ bajo el grifo/ mirando
          los montoncitos de tierra caer en el desagüe
hice un buen trabajo
me dijo agüela/ preparé bien esas verduras pa la olla
& sabes/ ningún hombre blanco en la tele/
hablando formal y bonito no entiende ná del milagro
de lo que me hace una buena olla de verduras un viernes de noche
es la única razón por laque los apago de la tele
no soporto sus chismes de las noticias/ posturas que no

from okra to greens

i haveta turn my television down sometimes cuz
i cant stand to have white people/ shout at me/
sometimes i turn it off
cuz i cant look at em in my bedroom either/
being so white
that's why i like/ greens/
they cdnt even smell you/ wdnt know what you taste like
without sneakin/ got no
idea you shd be tingled wit hot sauce & showered wit vinegar
yr pot liquor spread on hot rolls

i gotta turn the TV off cuz the white people
keep playing games/ & followin presidents on vacation at the war
there's too much of a odor problem on the TV too/ which
brings me back to greens

i remember my grandma at the market pickin turnips
collards kale & mustards/ to mix em up/ drop a ½ a strick a lean
in there wit some ham hock & oh my whatta life/
i lived in her kitchen/ wit greens i cd recollect
yes the very root of myself
  the dirt & lil bugs i looked for in the fresh collards/
  turnin each leaf way so slow/ under the spicket/ watchin
  lil mounds of dirt fall down the drain
i done a good job
grandma tol me/ got them greens just ready for the pot
& you know/ wdnt no white man on the TV/
talkin loud n formal make no sense of the miracle
a good pot a greens on a friday nite cd make to me
that's the only reason i turn em off the TV
cant stand they gosspin abt the news/ sides they dont

son nunca como los criminales & enemigos que a mí me gustan
por eso me gustan las VERDURAS/ sé cómo cocinar el verde
& puedo soñarlas bien/ mojando la salsita de la olla
& con aquellos pimientos //

never like the criminals & enemies i like anyway
that's why i like GREENS/ i know how to cook em
& i sure can dream gd/ soppin up the pot liquor
& them peppers and vinegar //

From *from okra to greens*

mi padre es un mago retirado
(para ifa, p.t. & bisa)

mi padre era un mago retirado
lo cual explica mi comportamiento irregular
tó salede sombreros mágicos
o de botellas sin fondo & los periquitos
se consiguen fácil como un par de conejos
o tres monedas de 50 centavos/ 1958

mi papi se retiró de la magia & se dedicó
a otro oficio porque este amigo mío
del 3er grado pidió ser blanco
de inmediato

qué podía hacer un mago americano de color que se respete asímismo
con una petición tan estrambótica/ cepto
abandonar toda esa abracadabra pata de cabra abra la casa tela de gaza
abra caverno lomo de cerdo   porque
los nenes de color que creen en la magia
eran políticamente peligrosos pala raza
& a ninguno lo iban a convertir en blanco
de inmediato   solo
del palmazo de las manos de mi papi

& la razón por laque soy tan peculiar
es que he estado estudiando la técnica de mi papi
& tó lo que hago es magia estos días
& es muy de color
muy ahora lo ves/ ahora
no te metas conmigo
                  vengo de una familia de hechiceros
retirados/ babalaos activos & videntes de poca monta
con 41 millones de criaturas espirituales & cuerpos celestes

my father is a retired magician

(for ifa, p.t. & bisa)

my father was a retired magician
which accounts for my irregular behavior
everythin comes outta magic hats
or bottles wit no bottoms & parakeets
are as easy to get as a couple a rabbits
or 3 fifty cent pieces/ 1958

my daddy retired from magic & took
up another trade cuz this friend of mine
from the 3rd grade asked to be made white
on the spot

what cd any self-respectin colored american magician
do wit such an outlandish request/ cept
put all them razzamatazz hocus pocus zippity-do-dah
thingamajigs away   cuz
colored chirren believin in magic
waz becomin politically dangerous for the race
& waznt nobody gonna be made white
on the spot   just
from a clap of my daddy's hands

& the reason i'm so peculiar's
cuz i been studyin up on my daddy's technique
& everythin i do is magic these days
& it's very colored
very now you see it/ now you
dont mess wit me
                    i come from a family of retired
sorcerers/ active houngans & pennyante fortune tellers
wit 41 million spirits critturs & celestial bodies

de nuestro lado
  escucharé sus problemas
  ayudaré con sus carreras sus amantes sus esposas
errantes
  haré la estancia de tu abuela en el cielo más gratificante
  aliviaré a tu madre en la menopausia & enseñaré atu hijo
  a limpiar su cuarto

SÍSÍSÍ   3 deseos es tó lo que hay
 cintas escarlata pa tu pelo
  bolas ben wa desde hong kong
   una miniatura de machu picchu

tó es posible
pero no hay ninguna maga de color en su sano juicio
que te hará blanca
 digo
  es magia negra
esto que ves
  & te pondré bonito y de color
& serás de color toa la vida
& te encantará/ eso deser de color/ toa la vida/ de color & te
 encantará
te encantará/ ser de color/

on our side
  i'll listen to yr problems
  help wit yr career   yr lover   yr wanderin spouse
  make yr grandma's stay in heaven more gratifyin
  ease yr mother thru menopause & show yr son
  how to clean his room

YES YES YES   3 wishes is all you get
  scarlet ribbons for yr hair
    benwa balls via hong kong
      a miniature of machu picchu

all things are possible
but aint no colored magician in her right mind
gonna make you   white
  i mean
    this is blk magic
you lookin at
    & i'm fixin you up good n colored
& you gonna be colored all yr life
& you gonna love it/ bein colored/ all yr life/ colored & love it
love it/ bein colored/

From *nappy edges*

11

para todos mis muertos y seres queridos
(para gail, tracie & viola)

qué vuá hacer con mis muertos
mis tumbas & mausoleos
estas plantas de maceta que dejan los extraños
sobretus ojos   cerrados
quizás sueñan   muertos/queridos
tan particularmente   no sé
qué hacer con ustedes

acaso los veré bailar/
sostener a tu hijo y preguntar/   cómo era mamá
debo acostarme contu esposo
quien te ve como una niña en mis memorias
tu madre   acaso me hablará en su seno hasta la muerte contigo
simula que noha sido ninguna madre
deja a un lado nuestras fantasías de smokey robinson
recuerdos que no llevan a ningún bien

agüela/ agüela
debo ir en auto con tus hijas a sentarnos
en el cementerio en días de sol/ desyerbarte
el útero/ no sería mejor si me quedara
en mi cocina/ haciendo gumbo/ frituras de bacalao
viendo *edge of night*/
restregándome las manos en el delantal/ tarareando
his eye is on the sparrow
en mi pared una foto tuya a los veinticinco
'ya habías entregado ala mujer/
nadie te conocería/ solo recordamos a mamá
cuando había más
no me acostaré toqueteando el amor de un hombre muerto
asando manzanas por un medallón relleno del pelo de

for all my dead & loved ones
(for gail, tracie & viola)

whatever shall i do with my dead
my tombs & mausoleums
these potted plants tended by strangers
over yr eyes   closed
maybe dreamin   dead/loved
so particularly   i dont know
what to do with you

shall i see you dancin/
hold yr child askin/   what's mommy like
should i sleep with yr husband
who sees yr childself in my memories
yr mother   will she bosom talk me to death with you
pretend she has been no mother
our smokey robinson fantasies set aside
recollections comin to no good end

grandma/ grandma
must i ride with yr daughters to sit
in the cemetery on sunny days/ weedin
yr womb/ wdnt it be better if i stayed
in my kitchen/ makin gumbo/ codfish cakes
watchin edge of nite/
rubbin my hands on my apron/ hummin
his eye is on the sparrow
yr photograph at 25 is on my wall
awready you had given yr woman over/
no one wd know you/ only mama is remembered
when waz there more
i shall not lie fondling a dead man's love
bakin apples for a locket jammed with hair from

una cabeza que ya no es arrogante
pero qué debo hacer
con mis muertos/ queridos tan particulares
que me dejan/ tan específicos

algunos no dejan de respirar
ala espera de besos
algunos desaparecen/ dan portazos a la salida
cuelgan el teléfono de golpe
uno se fue en una camioneta VW/ otro
me robó el sueño

me siento aquí a beberme las memorias
a entretener fantasmas/ añorando brazos
que ya no dan calor/ demasiado encantá
pa atender el pulso que me empuja pa
desprenderme de ustedes/ mis muertos y queridos

cuando conozco a un alguien/ tengo que saber
me rodeo de ustedes como una corte de videntes sagrados
si esta extraña ha de tener un espacio en mi vida
tiene que atraer sus espíritus hacia losde ella
porque a menudo me pregunto por momentos sobre los muertos
si quieres que hable
tienes que aprender la lengua de mis muertos y seres queridos
los he dejado atrás
una sobreviviente
a la espera de algo más

a head no longer arrogant
but what shall i do
with my dead/ loved so particularly
leavin me/ specifically

some never stop breathin
wantin kisses
some disappear/ slammin the door
bangin the phone
one went off in a VW bus/ another
stole my sleep

i sit here drinkin memories
entertainin ghosts/ longin for arms
no longer warm/ too enchanted
to tend the pulse pushin me on
to go off from you/ my dead & loved ones

when i meet a someone/ i must know
i place you round me like a court of holy seers
if this stranger is to have a space in my life
she must pull yr spirits to her own
for i wander regularly in moments of the dead
if you wd have me speak
you must learn the tongue of my dead & loved ones
i have been left behind
a survivor
holdin out for more

From *nappy edges*

alguna vez hubo bailes de cuarterones

alguna vez hubo bailes de cuarterones/ elegancia en st. louis/
   mulatos
de encaje/ jugando por tó el misisipi/ hacia memphis/ nueva
orleans y crepas de quimbombó cerca del bayou/ donde los pobres
   basura blanca
cantaban/ gemían/ tonos líquidos/ extraños/ por los pantanos/

once there were quadroon balls

once there were quadroon balls/ elegance in st. louis/ laced
mulattoes/ gamblin down the mississippi/ to memphis/ new
orleans n okra crepes near the bayou/ where the poor white trash
wd sing/ moanin/ strange/ liquid tones/ thru the swamps/

From *for colored girls who have considered suicide/ when the rainbow
is enuf*

tango

libre entre matorrales de pino
mi abuelo labró su finca
aprendió el yiddish pa limpiar las ventanas mejor
las ventanas francesas
las ventanas de dieciséis paneles
las ventanas de las terrazas
de un pueblo vedado
fabricó violines de pino
los barnizó los afinó
dejó quela música se llevara
a sus hijas del pueblo
lejos dela finca que
se quemó
pinos frondosos matorrales de pino
borran las ruinas del granero
las agujas de pino arañan el aire
cada vez quemi padre se limpia
las lágrimas de las mejillas
pero no de las ventanas
no había manchas
en las ventanas.

tango

loose in the brush pines
my grandfather farmed
learned yiddish to better wash windows
the french windows
the sixteen paned windows
the terraced windows
of a restricted town
he made violins of pine
varnished them tuned them
let music carry his daughters
out of the town
away from the farm that
burned down
scrubby pines brush pines
obliterate the ruins of the barn
the pine needles scratch the air
each time my father wipes the
tears from his cheeks
but not from the windows
there were never streaks
on the windows.

From *ridin' the moon in texas*

19

toussaint

la biblioteca estaba justo albajar los rieles del troli
frente a la lavandería
através de los pisos grandes y brillosos & los pilares de granito
que le dan fama a st. louis
encontré a toussaint
pero no después de meses de
cajun katie/ pipi lángstrun
christopher robin/ eddie heyward & un oso pú
en la sala pa niños
solo niñas pioneras & conejos mágicos
& nenes blancos de ciudades grandes
sabía que no se supone que pudiera
pero me colé en la SALA DE LECTURA PARA ADULTOS
                & me tropecé con

        TOUSSAINT
        mi primer afroamericano
(nunca conté a george washington carver
porque no me gusta el maní)
        y aun así
TOUSSAINT era un hombre negro un buen negro como decía mi
    mamá
que se rehusó a ser esclavo
& hablaba francés
& no doblaba el lomo ante el blanco pa decirle de ná
            ni a napoleón
            ni a maximillién
            ni a robespierre

TOUSSAINT L'OUVERTURE
era el principio dela realidá pa mí
en el concurso de verano pa ver
a quién pueden leer los niños de color

toussaint

de library waz right down from de trolly tracks
cross from de laundry-mat
thru de big shinin floors & granite pillars
ol st. louis is famous for
i found toussaint
but not til after months uv
cajun katie/ pippi longstockin
christopher robin/ eddie heyward & a pooh bear
in the children's room
only pioneer girls & magic rabbits
& big city white boys
i knew i waznt sposedta
but i ran into the ADULT READING ROOM
              & came across

      TOUSSAINT
       my first blk man
(i never counted george washington carver
cuz i didnt like peanuts)
       still
TOUSSAINT waz a blk man a negro like my mama say
who refused to be a slave
& he spoke french
& didnt low no white man to tell him nothin
          not napoleon
          not maximillien
          not robespierre

TOUSSAINT L'OUVERTURE
waz the beginnin uv reality for me
in the summer contest for
who colored children can read

15 libros en tres semanas
gané & despotriqué sobre TOUSSAINT L'OUVERTURE
y después dela ceremonia
me descualificaron
   porque TOUSSAINT
     pertenecía a la SALA DE LECTURA PARA ADULTOS
    & lloré
& me llevé a Toussaint muerto en el libro
estaba vivo y muerto pa mí
porque TOUSSAINT & ellos
juntos defendieron la ciudadela contra los franceses
conlos espíritus de africanos muertos de debajo de la tierra
TOUSSAINT dirigió un ejército de zombis
bola de cañón que camina y dispara espíritus pa liberar Haití
& nunca jamás de los jamases eran esclavos

      TOUSSAINT L'OUVERTURE
se hizo mi amante secreto cuando tenía 8 años
lo entretenía en mi cuarto
con la linterna entre mis sábanas
muy pero muy tarde en la noche/ discutíamos estrategias
cómo sacar a nenas blancas de mis juegos de rayuela
& etc.
TOUSSAINT
se acostaba en mi cama junto a la raggedy ann
la noche en que decidí escapar de mi
  casa integrada
   calle integrada
    escuela integrada
1955 no fue un buen año pa niñitas negras

Toussaint decía 'vámonos a haití'
yo dije 'dale'
& empaqué algunas cosas muy importantes en una bolsa de papel
 de estraza

15 books in three weeks
i won & raved abt TOUSSAINT L'OUVERTURE
at the afternoon ceremony
waz disqualified
       cuz TOUSSAINT
         belonged in the ADULT READING ROOM
          & i cried
& carried dead Toussaint home in the book
he waz dead & livin to me
cuz TOUSSAINT & them
they held the citadel gainst the french
wid the spirits of ol dead africans from outta the ground
TOUSSAINT led they army of zombies
walkin cannon ball shootin spirits to free Haiti
& they waznt slaves no more

             TOUSSAINT L'OUVERTURE
became my secret lover at the age of 8
i entertained him in my bedroom
widda flashlight under my covers
way inta the night/ we discussed strategies
how to remove white girls from my hopscotch games
& etc.
TOUSSAINT
waz layin in bed wit me next to raggedy ann
the night i decided to run away from my
     integrated home
       integrated street
         integrated school
1955 waz not a good year for lil blk girls

Toussaint said 'lets go to haiti'
i said 'awright'
& packed some very important things in a brown paper bag

pa no tener que volver
luego Toussaint & yo tomamos el tranvía de hodiamont
al río
última parada
solo 15 ¢
porque nadie podía ver a Toussaint cepto yo
& caminamos tó el norte de st. louis
donde solían vivir los franceses
en casitas de ladrillo toas pegaditas
apenas les faltaban ventanas & las tejas estaban disparejas
donde juegan niños de color & hay mujeres en los bajos
portales chupando cerveza

podía hablar con Toussaint allá por el río
aquí era dondenos iríamos de polizones
en un bote pa nueva orleans
& cogeríamos una yola pesquera pa puerto príncipe
luego solo íbamos a leer & hablar tó el tiempo
& comer bananos fritos
                    solo hablábamos & brincábamos por los viejos
                    borrachos
cuando este buen niño saltó a mi encuentro y me dijo
'MERA NENA MÁS TE VALE QUE VENGA A HABLAR CONMIGO'
bueno
miré a TOUSSAINT (que estaba enojao)
& le grité
'niño bobo
más vale queme dejes quieta
o TOUSSAINT te pateará el culo'
y el niño bobo dobló la esquina y se me rio en la cara
'oye nena jabá
debes ser alguien pa saber mi nombre tan rápido'
me dio asco
& quería seguir pa haití
sin ningún niño baboso molestando

so i wdnt haveta come back
then Toussaint & i took the hodiamont streetcar
to the river
last stop
only 15¢
cuz there waznt nobody cd see Toussaint cept me
& we walked all down thru north st. louis
where the french settlers usedta live
in tiny brick houses all huddled together
wit barely missin windows & shingles uneven
wit colored kids playin & women on low porches sippin beer

i cd talk to Toussaint down by the river
like this waz where we waz gonna stow away
on a boat for new orleans
& catch a creole fishin-rig for port-au-prince
then we waz just gonna read & talk all the time
& eat fried bananas
                         we waz just walkin & skippin past ol drunk
                    men
when dis ol young boy jumped out at me sayin
'HEY GIRL YA BETTAH COME OVAH HEAH N TALK TO ME'
well
i turned to TOUSSAINT (who waz furious)
& i shouted
'ya silly ol boy
ya bettah leave me alone
or TOUSSAINT'S gonna get yr ass'
de silly ol boy came round de corner laughin all in my face
'yellah gal
ya sure must be somebody to know my name so quick'
i waz disgusted
& wanted to get on to haiti
widout some tacky ol boy botherin me

pero se quedó ahí parao
pateaba cartones de leche & pedazos de ladrillo
intentaba entrometerse en mi camino
> le susurré a L'OUVERTURE 'qué debo
> hacer'
al final
le pregunté a este niño bobo
'¿QUIÉN ERES TÚ?'
me dijo
'ME LLAMO TOUSSAINT JONES'
bueno
lo miré fijo
aquellos pantalones de pana rasgados
la camisa rayada con rotos en los codos
un moretón nuevo sobre el ojo derecho
& le dije
> 'cómo es tu nombre otravez'
dijo
'es toussaint jones'
guau
voy de camino a ver
TOUSSAINT L'OUVERTURE en HAITÍ
acaso tienes algo quever con él
él no le aguanta zanganás a los blancos
& tienen un país pa ellos solos
& no son ningunos esclavos'
aquel niño bobo arrugó toa la cara
'mira pacá niña
soy TOUSSAINT JONES
& estoy aquí mirándote
& no le aguanto zanganás a los blancos
¿o acaso ves alguno por aquí?'
& como que sacó el pecho pa fuera
entonces dijo

still he kept standin there
kickin milk cartons & bits of brick
tryin to get all in my business
                        i mumbled to L'OUVERTURE 'what shd I do'
finally
i asked this silly ol boy
'WELL WHO ARE YOU?'
he say
'MY NAME IS TOUSSAINT JONES'
well
i looked right at him
those skidded cordoroy pants
a striped tee shirt wid holes in both elbows
a new scab over his left eye
& i said
                        'what's yr name again'
he say
'i'm toussaint jones'
'wow
i am on my way to see
TOUSSAINT L'OUVERTURE in HAITI
are ya any kin to him
he dont take no stuff from no white folks
& they gotta country all they own
& there aint no slaves'
that silly ol boy squinted his face all up
'looka heah girl
i am TOUSSAINT JONES
& i'm right heah lookin at ya
& i don't take no stuff from no white folks
ya dont see none round heah do ya?'
& he sorta pushed out his chest
then he say

'vente   bajemos a los muelles
a ver los barcos'

me sentía tan extraña bajando pa los muelles
con mi bolsa de papel & mis libros
y sentí que TOUSSAINT L'OUVERTURE como que me dejaba
& me sentí triste
hasta que me di de cuenta que
TOUSSAINT JONES no era muy distinto
de TOUSSAINT L'OUVERTURE
cepto que el viejo estaba en haití
& este conmigo me habla en inglés & come manzanas
ajá.
a mí me cae chévere este toussaint jones
no se sabe tós los espíritus que podríamos mover
abajo en el río
st. louis 1955   oye espera.

'come on   lets go on down to the docks
& look at the boats'

i waz real puzzled goin down to the docks
wit my paper bag & my books
i felt TOUSSAINT L'OUVERTURE sorta leave me
& i waz sad
til i realized
TOUSSAINT JONES waznt too different
from TOUSSAINT L'OUVERTURE
cept the ol one was in haiti
& this one wid me speakin english & eatin apples
yeah.
toussaint jones waz awright wit me
no tellin what all spirits we cd move
down by the river
st. louis 1955   hey wait.

From *for colored girls who have considered suicide/ when the rainbow
is enuf*

justo cuando los del vikings me robaron el corazón
(para tía emma)

mi hada madrina se retiró
con el fallo de *brown vs. ferguson*
pensó que yo me despojaba de ser separá
pero igual & que tenía derecho
alo que sea quele daban a las nenitas blancas
de quien sea que se lo dan
porque a ella la criaron en tierras más fértiles
& conocía el diablo solo en el aserrín azul
de un amanecer lascivo/ una danza cruel al filo de una moneda
así que se retiró/
no le gustaba eso de bastardear sus poderes/
tampoco eso de integrarlos/
y me dejó a valerme por mí misma

sentí su ausencia desde el momento en que se escapó
conmi amor por quien soy/ conjurarme
con piropos & petardos en el buzón no era mi fuerte
aprendí solo violando la ley/
   soy separá
   soy igual
vivo mi propia little rock/
me cubro las espaldas dondequiera que voy
& voy adonde yo quiera
los blanquitos nacen con derecho a vivir
yo me creo el mío
aquí en tu cara
   por qué no
    te atreves
& me empujas

just as the del vikings stole my heart

(for auntie emma)

my fairy godmother retired
with the brown vs. ferguson decision
she reasoned i waz divested of my separate
but equal status & waz entitled
to whatever lil white girls got
from whoever they got it from
since she waz raised in greener pastures
& knew the devil only in the blues saw-dust
of a raunchy dawn/ a cruel dance on the edge of a dime
so she retired/
she waznt bout to miscegenate her powers/
integrate em either/
leavin me to fend for myself

i've felt her absence from the moment she escaped
with my love of who i am/ conjurin myself
thru catcalls & mailbox cherry bombs was not my forte
i learned only by breakin the law/
        i am separate
        i am equal
i live my own lil rock/
cover my own back anywhere i wanna go
& i go anywhere i want
crackers are born with the right to be alive
i am making mine up
right here in your face
        why dont you
          go on
& push me

From *nappy edges*

31

sobre hacerme exitosa

"no parece lo sufisientemente afrikana pa' saber pero..."
"parece que chapotea en la vida del gueto..."

por qué no te atreves & integras una
escuela germano-americana en st. louis misuri/ 1955/ o mejor
por qué no te atreves a ser una india negrita en una escuela de
    negros en 1954/
lo tengo/ trata de hacer amigos en un campamento en los ozark en
    1957/
arrástrate por una desas cuevas de jessie james con una clase de
    niños blancos
que te esperan afuera pa ver el blanco de tus ojos/ por quéno
    invades
una pandilla de obreros italianos que intentan ser protestantes en
    una comunidá
judía/ y sé la espada de la baraja/ sé algo oscurito/ de labios muy
    carnosos/
de pelo completamente encaracolao/ sé hermoso/ sé un chico
    agusao que trata de ser
tonto/ tienes que conocer a alguien que quiere/ siempre/ un poco
    menos/ sé
templado cuando tu cuerpo dice caliente y más/ sé un error de
    integración racial/
un error en las fantasías más absurdas de los blancos/ sé una niña
    negra en 1954/
que no es lo sufisientemente negra pa ignorar con amor/ ni lo
    sufisientemente bella pa dejarla
quieta/ ni lo sufisientemente lista pa salirse del camino/ ni lo
    sufisientemente amargá pa morirse
joven/ por qué no vienes & vives mi vida por mí/ ya que los
poemas no son sufisientes/ atrévete & vive mi vida por mí/ no
    quería algunos momentos para nada
momentos después de tó/ se los daría a cualquiera/

on becomin successful

"she dont seem afrikan enuf to know bt . . ."
"seems she's dabblin in ghetto-life . . ."

why dont you go on & integrate a
german-american school in st. louis mo./ 1955/ better yet
why dont ya go on & be a red niggah in a blk school in 1954/
i got it/ try & make one friend at camp in the ozarks in 1957/
crawl thru one a jesse james' caves wit a class of white kids
waitin outside to see the whites of yr eyes/ why dontcha invade
a clique of working-class italians tryin to be protestant in a jewish
community/ & come up a spade/ be a lil too dark/ lips a lil too full/
hair entirely too nappy/ to be beautiful/ be a smart child tryin to be
dumb/ you go meet somebody who wants/ always/ a lil less/ be
cool when yr body says hot & more/ be a mistake in racial integrity/
an error in white folks' most absurd fantasies/ be a blk girl in 1954/
who's not blk enuf to lovinly ignore/ not beautiful enuf to leave
alone/ not smart enuf to move outta the way/ not bitter enuf to die
at a early age/ why dontcha c'mon & live my life for me/ since the
poems aint enuf/ go on & live my life for me/ i didnt want certain
moments at all/ i'd give em to anybody/

From *nappy edges*

rizos de caracol (un viaje por todo el país)

st. louis/ un pueblo tan de color/ un espacio de la historia
y vecindario color whiskey negro/ pa siempre nuestro/
a lawrenceville/ donde hay solo una carretera abierta
pa mí/ salvada por esclavos coloniales/ cuyos hijos nunca
se mudaron/ parece que nunca/ repararon los tormentos de la
Depresión
las manchas de saliva demente/ que cayó de los labios de mujeres
de cristal/
que aún fabrican banderas de independencia/
de st. louis/ en una víspera de halloween al baile del profeta
velado/
que usurpa el misterio del mardi gras/ lo hice mío aunque la reina
siempre era justa/ aquel desfile/ de carrozas flotantes & panderetas/
que me conmemoran a mí/ contrario a las caminatas con niños
disfrazados
liberales/ hasta mi puerta principal/ la bolsa medio vacía/
mi cara lo sufisiente pa asustar a tó aquel que pasa/ un niño
de color/
qué risa

    1) aquí
      un árbol
      deambulando el horizonte
      inmerso en huesos
      desatendidos & azules
      acostumbrao a abrazos acentos
      ritmo & decencia
      aquí un árbol
      esperando aque lo ahorquen

la secundaria sumner/ acuclillada & pálida en la esquina/ como
nuestra visión/ iba a ser vaga/ nuestra memoria

nappy edges (a cross country sojourn)

   st. louis/ such a colored town/ a whiskey
black space of history & neighborhood/ forever ours/
   to lawrenceville/ where the only road open
to me/ waz cleared by colonial slaves/ whose children never
moved/ never seems like/ mended the torments of the Depression
the stains of demented spittle/ dropped from lips of crystal women/
still makin independence flags/
   from st. louis/ on a halloween's eve to the veiled prophet/
usurpin the mystery of mardi gras/ made it mine tho the queen
waz always fair/ that parade/ of pagan floats & tambourines/
commemoratin me/ unlike the lonely walks wit liberal trick or
treaters/ back to my front door/ bag half empty/
   my face enuf to scare anyone i passed/ a colored kid/
whatta gas

   1) here
        a tree
        wanderin the horizon
        dipped in blues &
        untended bones
        usedta hugs drawls
        rhythm & decency
        here a tree
        waitin to be hanged

   sumner high school/ squat & pale on the corner/ like
our vision/ waz to be vague/ our memory

de la guerra/ que nos hizo libres pa ser olvidados
se hizo más pálida/ un movimiento linear de carolina del sur
a misuri/ los liberados/ aterrizaron en el aullido de jackie wilson/
    hijas de
los libertos nadando en el meneo de tina turner/ este es el pueblo
    de chuck
berry/ mestizaje renegado/ en cualquier situación/ & nos
dejan ser/ un blues eléctrico & la hipocresía de bo diddley/ que
    roquea pulmonía
& influenza *boogie-woogie*/ bazofia & cabecitas fritas/ que corren
    siempre al
río

              / de chambersbourg/ la pequeña italia/ pasaba tós los días
por la tienda de dulces/ & tenía miedo/ los guardias asaltaban a los
    vagos/
a menudo/ cae la noche & yano me verán/ con algún otro de color/
sensata/ amando mi vida/
            en el 'bourg/ esperando en serio a queme retuerzan/
oye negra/ ven acá/
            & detrás del camión yacen cinco manos que abrochan cadenas/
por los árboles/ 4 más maman acero

                                    oye maldita negra/ ven
    acá/
esta es la frontera/
una disputa territorial/

                                    oye maldita negra/
ven acá/
        carros cargados de familias/ los muchachos de la factoría/ una
            o dos
enfermeras prácticas/ negras/ son nuestras trincheras/ algunas
    cavan en el cemento
con los codos/ debajo de los motores/ queno te vean/ en tu pueblo/
    después
del atardecer chupamos nuestras sombras/

of the war/ that made us free to be forgotten
becomin paler/ a linear movement from south carolina
to missouri/ freedmen/ landin in jackie wilson's yelp/ daughters of
the manumitted swimmin in tina turner's grinds/ this is chuck
berry's town/ disavowin miscega-nation/ in any situation/ & they let
us be/ electric blues & bo diddley's cant/ rockin pneumonia &
boogie-woogie flu/ the slop & short-fried heads/ running always to
the river

　　　/ from chambersbourg/ lil italy/ i passed everyday
at the sweet shoppe/ & waz afraid/ the cops raided truants/
regularly/ after dark i wd not be seen/ wit any other colored/
sane/ lovin my life/
　　　in the 'bourg/ seriously expectin to be gnarled/
hey niggah/ over here/
　　　& behind the truck lay five hands claspin chains/
round the trees/ 4 more sucklin steel/

　　　　　　　　　　　　hey niggah/ over here
this is the borderline/
a territorial dispute/

　　　　　　　　　　　　hey/ niggah/
over here/
　　　cars loaded wit families/ fellas from the factory/ one or two
practical nurses/ black/ become our trenches/ some dig into cement
wit elbows/ under engines/ do not be seen/ in yr hometown/ after
sunset we suck up our shadows/

2) me sentaré aquí
mis hombros abrazan un roble enorme
los sueños se balancean en mi falda
por donde miz bertha donde little richard
consigue su proceso
corre patrás a los rosales/ un borracho/ acostado
manzana abajo a las monjas de hábito rosao
que oran en una capilla rosá
mis sueños corren a conocer a la tía marie
mis sueños sacan sangre de viejas heridas
estas marcas & cicatrices son mías
este es mi espacio
de aquí no me muevo

2) i will sit here
    my shoulders brace an enormous oak
    dreams waddle in my lap
    round to miz bertha's where lil richard
    gets his process
    run backwards to the rosebushes/ a drunk man/ lyin
    down the block to the nuns in pink habits
    prayin in a pink chapel
    my dreams run to meet aunt marie
    my dreams draw blood from ol sores
            these stains & scars are mine
                this is my space
                    i am not movin

From *nappy edges*

39

escuché a eric dolphy en sus ojos

ayer caída la tarde/ no/ más bien anoche/ la
luna tomó un matiz escarlata/ *lune rouge/ luna*
roja/ una luna loca/ soy yo una loquita/ *
através de las brumas & las nubes que se mezclan
con invitaciones de neón & lágrimas sin derramar/lágrimas
que esperan el mañana/ alcancé el tren expreso
IRT en la 7ma avenida/ personalizado pa el bulevar Malcolm X
& los abanicos de colores a computadora del
Schomburg/ el tren silbaba a su paso/ de lujo
desde la calle 145/ hasta mi corazón/ palpitaba
& buscaba ritmos que se acoplan a vientos
helados & al esmog quese mezcla con el neón &
las nubes/ merodean/ la base de los hidrantes
las piernas feroces y descarás de las jóvenes que procuran
su propia perdición/
        "Ra, Ra"
digo/ es esto un juego de fútbol americano
        "Ra, Ra"

digo/ los Knicks deben estar jugando en la
calle 155/ enel lugar habitual de la noche/
        "Ra, Ra"
la marcha/ se mueve hacia Howard Beach/
otro día/ de indignación/
        "Ra, Ra"
debe ser Daniel Ortega/ o Fidel/ atrás
en una terraza/ con confeti y plumas
de gallina/ ovaciones de absolución/
ovaciones/ que proclaman la llegada/ de
un nuevo día/

---

* Translator's note: Italicized verses are in French and Spanish, respectively, in the
original.

i heard eric dolphy in his eyes

yesterday evenin/ no/ mo like last night/ the
moon took on a scarlet hue/ *lune rouge/ luna*
roja/ una luna loca/ soy yo una loquita/
thru mists & the clouds that mix
wit neon invitations & tears unshed/ tears
waitin for tomorrow/ i met the 7th Avenue IRT
Express/ specially tailored for Malcolm X Boulevard
& the computerized palettes at the
Schomburg/ the train came whistling by/ deluxe
from 145th Street/ to my heart/ throbbin
& seekin rhythms not uncomfortable wit wind
chill factors & smog what cd mix wit neon &
cloud/ hoverin/ by the base of hydrants
ferocious brazen legs of young girls seein to
their own undoin/
    "Rah, Rah"
i says/ is this a football game
    "Rah, Rah"

i says/ the Knicks must be playin at
155th Street/ in the chill spill of the night/
    "Rah, Rah"
the march/ is movin on to Howard Beach/
another day/ of outrage/
    "Rah, Rah"
must be Daniel Ortega/ or Fidel/ back
on a terrace/ wit confetti & chicken
feathers/ cheers of absolution/
cheers/ proclaimin the comin/ of
a new day/

           "Ra, Ra"
llega una voz/ que vapulea/ como un
buldócer/ llega una voz muy acostumbrada al dolor/
           "Ra, Ra"
el tambaleo de un niño/ de un poste a
otro/ su abrigo de nieve asqueroso y rasgado
más acostumbrado/ a que lo escupan
que a trazar ángeles en la nieve/ el frío muerde sus
piecitos desnudos/ llora/ este bebé que apenas
puede caminar/ pero lo cierto es
que es muy joven/ llora y sonríe
al mismo tiempo/ sordo a su propio nombre/
           "Ra, Ra"
           "jodío negro/ levántate del piso/ ¿me oíste?
           lebanta ese culo negro del suelo/ jodío negro/ ¿me oíste?"
al niño/ Ra Ra/ lo deberían
alabar/ se esfuerza tanto/ lo intenta
lo intenta/ con esfuerzo/ alcanza/ con sus
bracitos el plástico duro y gris del
banco del metro/ levanta sus pies manchados
de rosa/ del piso/ pero/ no lo bastante rápido
porque la voz/ esa penetrante y
cruda/ y repugnante voz/ sigue al acecho del
niño/ arriba & arriba & arriba/ hasta el asiento/ &
luego/ el pobre niño se cae patrás/ encima
de la sección de tirillas del *Daily News*/ la
página de opinión del *Times*/ los clasificados de *The Advocate*/
& misceláneos/ oportunidades espirituales destacás en
el *Amsterdam News*/ que proclaman que solo
un/ Eleguá visita a Harlem cada
año/ & solo un/ amor podría salvarnos de
la desgracia/ & solo un/ niño fue
alzado por el trasero del pantalón/ boca
abajo en aquel banco repleto de

    "Rah, Rah"
come a voice/ pummelin/ like a
bulldozer/ come a voice too usedta pain/
    "Rah, Rah"
the child's tumblin/ from one pole to
the next/ his filthy tattered snowsuit
mo accustomed/ to bein spat on/
than makin angels/ the cold nibbles his
naked lil feet/ he cries/ this baby who can
barely walk/ cuz he simply
is too young/ now/ the child cries & smiles
at the same time/ deaf to his own name/
    "Rah, Rah"
    "niggah/ get up off da floor/ ya heah me?
    git yo black ass off da floor/ niggah/ ya heah me?"
the child/ RahRah/ shoulda been
praised/ he tries so hard/ he tries
he tries/ so hard/ he reaches/ wit his lil
arms for the hard grey plastic of the
subway bench/ he pulls his pink-smudged feet
up/ offa the ground/ but/ not fast enough
cuz the voice/ that barrelin
crude/ nasty ol voice/ keeps chasin the
child/ up & up & up/ to the seat/ &
then/ the po child falls back down/ on
top the comic strips from the *Daily News*/ the
Times OpEd page/ the personals from *The Advocate*/
& miscellaneous/ spiritual opportunities featured in
the *Amsterdam News*/ proclaimin that only
one/ Papa Legbé visited Harlem each
year/ & only one/ love could save us from
misfortune/ & only one/ child was
hoisted by the seat of his pants/ nose
first down on the hard littered

basura/ donde la mano de la voz
del puño de un hijueputa barriobajero
se enterró en la carne y médula de un niño
que apenas podía hablar/ o caminar/ que ha dominao
el arte de sollozar & sonreír/ al mismo
tiempo/ un niño que alza los brazos como
si fuera a abrazar la voz/
        "Ra, Ra"
mira/ a tóel mundo/
los puños/ rebotan de sus
sienes a sus pantorrillas/ sonríe &
llora/ desea/ quizás desea/ en este
momento/ que la voz nole quite la gorra
negra y sucia/ de su cabeza de costra y caracol/ desea
que las manos de la voz/ no le enrollen/
las piernas del pantalón/ ahí sí que no habría forma de repeler
el frío/ espera que la pandereta/ no esté
puesta encima de su cochecito/ puesta por la voz/
se quita sus propios zapatos pa balancearse/ en
una pierna de madera/ se apoya en ella
cuando no le pegan/
        "Ra Ra"
                    "vamu'acel mucha plata
                    hoy/ vamu'a encendernos/
                    oh sí/ sí/ sí hoy/
                    hoy/
                    me vuá/ encender/
                    hoy"
& pum/ por la cabeza del bebé con
los nudillos/ que deja un chichón
que sangra/ bajo el ojo derecho/
& el bebé trata de sonreír/
                    "damas & caballeros/ aquí vivimo
                    en la calle & queríamo que nos

bench/ where the hand of the voice
the fist of the low-down muthafuckah
crashed into the flesh & marrow of a child
who can barely talk/ or walk/ who has mastered
the art of weepin & smilin/ at the
same time/ a child who raises his arms like
he gonna hug the voice/
      "Rah, Rah"
he's lookin/ at all of us/
the fists/ ricochet off his
temple to his calves/ smilin &
cryin/ wishin/ maybe wishin/ this heah
time/ the voice won't take his dirty red
hat/ offa his scabby nappy head/ wishin
the hands of the voice/ wouldn't roll his/
pants legs up/ so wazn't no way to fend off
the cold/ hopin a tambourine/ wouldn't be
set on top his stroller/ by the voice/
takin off his own shoes to balance/ on
a wooden leg/ he leans on it
when he's not beatin/
      "RahRah"
                "we gonna make some money
                tonight/ we gonna git fired up/
                awright/ yeah/ yeah tonight/
                tonight/
                gone git me/ all fired up/
                tonight"
& whack/ cross the baby's head wit
knuckles/ leavin a puffed up
bleedin space/ neath the right eye/
& the baby tries to smile/
                "ladies & gentlemen/ we heah is
                homeless & we'd like ya to give

diesen/ lo que sea que el señol les
diga/ saben cómo son lo muchacho/
avece/ hay que sel un poco
duro con ellos"
háblame/ Ra Ra/ háblame
Ra Ra/ quiero cantarte hasta
queno haya más niebla por el lago michigan/
hasta que/ no haya más cacofonía de metal
sobre tu cabeza/ tedejaré
respirar algo tierno/ como el rocío/ aire
fresco & alguien tierno que cuide tu
entorno/ por tós lados/ juro que oí a A.I.R.E
triunfar delicada/en sus ojos/
ternura en sus ojos/ feroz/ en sus ojos
digo/ oí una canción de A.I.R.E.

oí una canción de A.I.R.E. en sus ojos/
Ra Ra/ Ra Ra/
oí por favor/ en sus suspiros
oí/ qué te he hecho/ en sus ojos
Ra Ra/ Ra Ra/
levántate/ juye por tu vida/

ahí en sus ojos en la cruel
noche/ el rastro de murmullos & risitas malas
dirigían a un fagot solista/ a
un clarinete bajo/ un sonido más amplio más
poderoso/ que este niño/ lo sé/ lo oí
Chicago aúlla por sus ojos/ cuando
el amor emerge como migajas/ se
va a levantar & sonreirá/ sabía que estabaquí
tóel tiempo/ estabaquí/ como
yo/ incompleto & frágil/ como una canción de
A.I.R.E./ que mece/ la tristeza/

_____

                    us/ whatever the lord moves ya
                    to do/ ya know how kids are/
                    sometimes/ ya gotta be a lil
                    hard on em"
speak to me/ RahRah/ speak to me
RahRah/ i wanna sing to ya til
there's no mo fog round lake michigan/
til there's/ no mo steely cacophony
just above yo head/ let ya
breathe somethin tender/ like dew/ fresh
air & someone tenderly round bout
ya/ everywhere/ i swear i heard A.I.R.
delicately triumph/ in his eyes/
tender in his eyes/ fierce/ in his eyes
i say/ i heard an A.I.R. song

i heard A.I.R. in his eyes/
RahRah/ RahRah/
i heard please/ in his sighs
i heard/ what'd i ever do to you/ in his eyes
RahRah/ RahRah/
Get up/ run for yo life/

there in his eyes in the harsh
night/ trail of whimpers & mean giggles
led a solo bassoon/ a
bass clarinet/ some sound broader mo
powerful/ than this child/ i know/ i heard
Chicago howlin thru his eyes/ when
love surfaces like crumbs/ he's
gone set up & grin/ i knew ya were heah
all along/ ya were heah/ like
me/ unfinished & frail/ like an A.I.R.
song/ rockin/ sadness/

———

quiero saber/ cómo suena el amor/

quiero saber/ cómo suena el amor

A.I.R.E./ aire fresco/ A.I.R.E. nuevo/ en sus ojos/

Ra Ra/ Ra Ra/

oigo un no me pegues otra vez sabe

en sus ojos/ frío o noche/ en sus ojos/

Ra Ra/ Ra Ra/

oí a eric dolphy en sus ojos/

> "damas & caballeros/ aquí vivimo
> en la calle & queríamos que nos
> diesen/ lo que sea que el señol les
> diga/ saben cómo son lo muchacho/
> avece/ hay que ser un poco
> duro con ellos"

i wanna know/ what love sounds like/
i wanna know/ what love sounds like
A.I.R./ fresh air/ new A.I.R./ in his eyes/
Rah Rah/ Rah Rah/
i hear don't hit me again awright
in his eyes/ cold or night/ in his eyes/
RahRah/ RahRah/
i heard eric dolphy in his eyes/

> "ladies & gentlemen/ we heah is
> homeless & we'd like ya to give
> us/ whatever the lord moves ya
> to do/ ya know how kids are/
> sometimes/ ya gotta be a lil
> hard on em"

From *the love space demands*

se busca chica con esperiensia

—de un cartel en una ventana de la ciudad de Nueva York,
calle 20 entre las avenidas 9 y 10

1)
quévas jacer
con toas esas
sémolas de-mo-te, nena
nosabes que
arriba al norte
los negros
no comen ninguna sémola frita
comemos
pan... quequos
de arándano
como en la casa de los panqueques
hay algunos tontos
que se creen africanos comiendo arroz & to eso
pero no molehtan a nadie
no si no quieren decir ná

2)
pasa la sal, esa de ahí beba
quiero echarle sal
a estos huevos con sémola
eh nena
aonde está mi cuenta
no pue'es ir más deprisa
subes pacá y se te olvida cómo actuar
si fueze hombre blanco
coooooño si fueze hombre blanco
apuestoaque brincas
sobre la barra esa
con gana de darme

expiriese girl wanted

—from a sign in a New York City window, 20th Street
between 9th and 10th Avenues

1)
whatchu gonna do
wid all them
ho-mo-ny grits, gal
donchu know
up north
niggahs
don' eat no fried grits
we eat blueberry
pan . . . cakes
like at the pan cake house
there is some fools
think they african eatin rice & shit
but they don't bothah nobody
naw they don' mean a thing

2)
pass the salt, please there honey
i wanta put some salt
on these eggs 'n grits
hey girl
where's my check
cantchu move no fastern that
come up heah 'n forget how to act
if i waz a white man
sheeeeit   if i waz a white man
i betchu wd jump
cross that counter
wantin to gimme

algún cantito
desa chocha pelúa
ah, nena

3)
te vi con ese tipo
PUM PUM   baaaaaaaaaaam
                    AAAAAAAA aaaaaaaaaaayyy
te digo que te vi
le tenías las tetas atragantás
PUM PUM PUM
                    AAAAAAAA aaaaa ay beba
te lo vuá decir otra vez
PUM PUM
no pue'es vender lo que no es tuyo
PUM PUM
to lo que tengas
PUMMMMMMMM PUM bam bam PUMMMMMMMMMMMMmmmmmm
                    JAAAAAAAAAAAAYaaaaaaaaaaay
to lo que tengas/ nena/ es mío
PUM PUM   tú sabe
siéntate y calla

4)
te digo
ese negro'e un descarao
trayendo a esa puta aquí   a mi casa
esa no eh'más que un
boquete grande con las uñas pintás
sé que ella no pue'e calentarlo
como lo hago yo/ sé lo que hay que hacer con eso
nena/ lo conozco bien
ademá
ninguna chocha es de oro

some of that there
bushy pussy
huh, gal

3)
i seen ya wid that dude
BLAM BLAM   baaaang
                    OOOOOOOO oooooooh
i say i seen ya
tits pushed halfway down his throat
BLAM BLAM BLAM
                    OOOOOO oooo oh honey
i aint gonna tell you again
BLAM BLAM
ya cant sell what aint yours 'n
BLAM BLAM
everything you got
BLAMMMMM BLAM bang bang BLAMMMMMMMmmmm
                    HOOOOOOOOOooooooooooooh
everything you got/ girl/ is mine
BLAM BLAM   ya understand
sit down 'n shut up

4)
i'm tellin ya
that niggah's got some nerve
bringin that bitch up heah   in my house
she aint nothin but a
big ol hole wit painted fingernails
i know she cant get him off
like i can/ i know just what to do wit that stuff
girl/ i know that man
'sides
aint nobody's cunt golden

5)

sí, mami

me encanta nueva yol

sí, mami

tengo un buen trabajo

ajá, en un restaurante

viene gente mu' buena acá

ajá y me dan buenas propinas

tós me tratan bien chévere

& ma, vuá mandar a buscarte a ti y a papi

tan pronto ya me sepa mover

   y me acostumbre a

     acostumbre a...

5)

yeah, mama
i like new york fine
yeah, mama
i gotta real nice job
uh huh, in a restaurant
real nice folks come there
uh huh i get good tips
everybody's been treatin me real nice
& i'ma send for you 'n daddy
soon as i get to know my way roun'
   'n get usedta
     usedta . . . . .

From *nappy edges*

dama de azul

solía vivir en el mundo
luego me mudé a HARLEM
& mi universo es ahora seis cuadras

cuando caminé en el pacífico
imaginé aguas antiguas como acra/ túnez
me limpia/ mealimenta
ahora a mis tobillos los cubre un sucio verde
del charco bajo el hidrante

mis océanos eran mi vida
qué aguas tengo aquí aún estancadas
circulando los cuerpos de hombres viejos
mierda & botellitas rotas de whiskey
dejadas pa hacerme sangrar

solía vivir en el mundo
ahora vivo en harlem & mi universo es seis cuadras
un túnel con un tren
puedo irme a cualquier parte
y seguiré siendo una extraña

lady in blue

i usedta live in the world
then i moved to HARLEM
& my universe is now six blocks

when i walked in the pacific
i imagined waters ancient from accra/ tunis
cleansin me/ feedin me
now my ankles are coated in grey filth
from the puddle neath the hydrant

my oceans were life
what waters i have here sit stagnant
circlin ol men's bodies
shit & broken lil whiskey bottles
left to make me bleed

i usedta live in the world
now i live in harlem & my universe is six blocks
a tunnel with a train
i can ride anywhere
remaining a stranger

From *for colored girls who have considered suicide/ when the rainbow
is enuf*

toma el tren A

podría dormir con un hombre
pero meacostaré con las almas de los negros
quizás podría cosecharme algo
alguna flor celeste que me huela
a la vida/ una raíz dealguna especia sanadora
podría brotar demis suelos/ si
duermo con las almas de los negros.

lo que es invisible no es un hombre
sino los espíritus de algunos que eran
más grande no es un niño negro que anhela un avión
sino la mirada de nuestros niños que no saben
por qué 'no consiguen satisfacción'
como cantaba otis.

podría dormir con un hombre
podría incluso cantar con un hombre
pero tengo que levantarme con las almas de los negros
adonde pueda llevarme el tren A
si no sé adónde se supone que vaya
ellington no es una calle
       & mi niña sabe que   su mundo
       es tan rico como *las personas en pena* pueden aportar/
       impetuosas como nuestros cuerpos en el *bosque negro*

pero no siempre hasido de esta manera
lo juro/ no siempre estábamos desaparecidos.

take the A train

i could sleep with a man
but i'll lay with the souls of black folks
maybe i could grow me something
some azure flower that would smell
like life to me/ a root of some healing spice
might push up from my soils/ if i
dream with the souls of black folks.

what is invisible is not a man
but the spirits of some who were
bigger is not a black boy yearning for an airplane
but the gaze of our children who dont know
why 'we caint get no satisfaction.'

i could sleep with a man
i could even sing with a man
but i gotta rise with the souls of black folks
where could the A train take me
if i dont know where im sposed to go
ellington is not a street.
      & my child knows   her world
          is as rich as *people in sorrow* can spare/
          brash as our bodies in the *black forest*

but it hasnt always been this way
i swear/ we were not always missing.

From *a daughter's geography*

sueño de apareamiento

sueño con copular
& descubro al extraño que se hará uno conmigo
sueño toda la noche con este hombre
su rostro cambia pero siempre está lleno de amor
pa mí / a veces logro tomarle la mano
una vez bailamos en Xenon's al ritmo de LaBelle
pero pueden haber sido los hermanos Jackson
me lanzó sobre su cabeza & me asió
entre sus piernas como aquellos que bailaban
el *jitterbug* en la SGM / de la forma en que George
Faison lo hacía en el Magique en el 25º aniversario
de Motown / nunca le permití que
me besara / él quería / este extraño
que me visita en mis sueños / pero eso
sería demasiado personal / él nunca
me dijo su nombre.

dream of pairing

i dream of coupling
discovering the stranger who'd be one with me
i dream all night long of this man
his face changes but is always full of love
for me / sometimes i manage to hold his hand
once we danced at Xenon's to LaBelle
but it might have been the Jacksons
he threw me over his head & drew
me tween his legs like those old
WWII jitter buggers / the way George
Faison did at Magique on Motown's 25th
anniversary party / i've never let
him kiss me / he wanted to / this stranger
who visits me in my dreams / but that
would be too personal / he's never
told me his name.

From *ridin' the moon in texas*

dama de azul II

algoque no necesito
es más disculpas
tengo a perdón saludándome ami puerta
puedes quedarte los tuyos
noséqué hacer con ellos
no abren puertas
no regresan el sol
nome hacen feliz
ni buscan el periódico
no hay ninguno que dejara de usar mis lágrimas pa lavar autos
por un perdón

lady in blue II

one thing i dont need
is any more apologies
i got sorry greetin me at my front door
you can keep yrs
i dont know what to do wit em
they dont open doors
or bring the sun back
they dont make me happy
or get a mornin paper
didnt nobody stop usin my tears to wash cars
cuz a sorry

From *for colored girls who have considered suicide/ when the rainbow
is enuf*

mucho cuerpo & herencia cultural/

puedo hablar   hablar contigo
como los spinners hablaban de un
            AMOR PODEROSO
            AMOR PODEROSO PODEROSO PODEROSO PODEROSO
eso me atrapa
    pienso en negro y me doy cuenta
de color
que no soporto que ningún tipo me llamé *BEIBI*
a la cara/
    pero si escucho un estilizado du-uá/
acaso nosabes que te la quiero soltar
BEIBIIIIII ME HACES SENTIR TAN NUEVO
sentirme nueva
& hay otro pavoneo con el que no puedo vivir
trajes de satén & mancuernas flojas
    camisas de crepé azul volcán & pechos fornidos
como mohamed alí ido & educado
            pa cautivar a una dama
                convertir una niña en mujer desde el escenario
                poner la jeva a gritar
                    & ella no sabe el nombre de ese hombre
UÉ-UÁ-UÉ-UÁ-ÉU-UÁ-ÓU-JAAAAAAAAAAAAAaaaaaaaaa
la audacia del blues

            roquéame papi
        revuélcame   papi
        dame rock n roll en la joyita

lotsa body & cultural heritage/

can i have a word   the word wid you
like the spinners waz talkin bout a
         MIGHTY LOVE
     MIGHTY MIGHTY MIGHTY MIGHTY LOVE
that grabs me
  i'm thinkin black and realizin
colored
cant stand no man to be callin me *BABEE*
to my face/
   but if i hear some stylistics du-wah/
donchu know i wanna give it away
BABEEEEEEEEE YOU MAKE ME FEEL SO BRAND NEW
feel brand new
& there's another strut i cant do widout
satiné suits & lamé cuffs
   volcano blue crepe shirts & heavy chests
like muhammad ali gone & learned
      to charm a lady
          sweep a child to womanhood from the stage
          make mama scream
            & she don't know that man's name
UE-WAH-UE-WAH-EU-WAH-OW-HAAAAAAAaaaaa
the audacity of the blues

       rock me daddy
  roll me   daddy
  rock n roll me at the bijou

From *nappy edges*

suelta las cuerdas o dame un "la"

sí/ escuché a country joe & the fish/
    sí/ aullé con steppenwolf/
sí/ fleetwood mac era mi epifanía/
    & creedence clearwater revival
me arrebató bajo las aguas/   hendrix
mi himno nacional siempre/   sí
    blind lemon jefferson & b.b. huddle
por la puerta de mi escenario/ sí chuck berry vive
junto a mí/   sí
      eric clapton me hizo desear tener
            una niña llamada layla/ sí
sonny sharrock me sacó gritos de la garganta
          que linda no puede eclipsar/
sí/ recuerdo la debacle de My Lai & la de Audubon
sí/ hamza-el-din es un caracol que me sale de la boca
sí/ nunca olvidé de dónde vengo &
a nadie le hago falta porque/
          nunca me fui
  en busca de un retrato
       o de un artista
         cuando era un hombre joven/
sí   leí el ULISES & regresó a casa
      sí/ ay/ sí
                conozco mi/ Joyce
podría identificar los acordes negros queme dejó/
sí/ "Busco... Busco"/ Me dicen mis olímpicos
Circe/ Escila Caribdis/
         cualquier sirena & tóel Pentágono
sí/ Circe/ Escila/ Caribdis,
     cualquier Sirena/ y tóel Pentágono/
nohan podido/ sí/ tedigo/ nohan podido
impedir que este/ sí/ queste negro/ sí

loosening strings or give me an 'A'

yes/ i listened to country joe & the fish/
    yes/ i howled with steppenwolf/
yes/ fleetwood mac was my epiphany/
    & creedance clearwater revival
swept me neath the waters/   hendrix
my national anthem always/   yes
    blind lemon jefferson & b.b. huddle
by my stage door/ yes chuck berry lives
next to me/   yes
        eric clapton made me wanna have
                a child named layla/   yes
sonny sharrock drew screams outta me
                linda can't eclipse/
yes/ i remember My Lai & the Audubon debacle
yes/ hamza-el-din is a caracole out my mouth
yes/ i never forgot where i came from &
nobody misses me cuz/
                  i never left
    in search of a portrait
        of an artist
            as a yng man/
yes   i read ULYSSES & he came home
                yes/ oh/ yes
                    i know my/ Joyce
i cd tell niggah chords meant for me/
yes/ "I'm searchin . . . I'm searchin"/ my Olympics say
Circe/ the Scylla the Charybdis/
                any Siren & all the Pentagon
yes/ Circe/ the Scylla/ the Charybdis,
    any Siren/ and alla the Pentagon/
aint kept/ yes/ i say/ aint kept
this one/ yes/ niggah man/ from/ yes

                    haga arte de mí/
sí/
        "lo vuámar completito/ completo/
                & una & otra vez"
porque los negros no están enbuscade /
        nosotras/ nos descubren
así que/ sí
    debo de estar en el Nuevo Mundo ahora/ sí
estoy en una melodía
ay/ sí/ tócame
                    acóplate/ a mis tonos de color
    sí/ rasguea mis cuerdas/ negras
                    encuentra/ mis bemoles & sostenidos
déjales/ algo/ de espacio
ay/ sí ay/ sí/ conozco mi Joyce
& mi Ulises/ sí que vino pa casa
sí/ tócame/ ahora
sí/ hazme toeso
sí/ me pondré debajo o podría solo montar
sí/ conozco mi Joyce/ & tolo que tienes quedecir/ es
        "Dame un 'la'"
        Aaaaaaaaaaaaaaaaaaaaaaaaaaa
sí/ Ulises sí que vino pa casa
sí/ debo estar en el Nuevo Mundo
sí/ Ulises sí que vino pa casa
sí/ debo estar en el Nuevo Mundo
sí/ estoy en sintonía
solo sí/ ay sí/ solo tócame
    papi/ tócame/
                sí/

makin art outta me/
yes/
         "i'm gonna love him all over/ all over/
                  & over & over"
cuz niggahs aint in search of /
      we/ just get discovered
so/ yes
    i must be in the New World now/ yes
i'm in tune
oh/ yes/ play me
                     pick/ my colored tones
      yes/ strum my niggah/ chords
                  find/ my sharps & flats
let em/ have/ space
oh/ yes oh/ yes/ i know my Joyce
& Ulysses/ he done come home
yes/ play me/ now
yes/ make me alla that
yes/ i'll be the bottom or i cd just ride
yes/ i know my Joyce/ & all you gotta say/ is
         "Give me a 'A' "
         Ahhhhhhhhhhhhhhhh
yes/ Ulysses he done come home
yes/ i must be the New World
yes/ Ulysses he done come home
yes/ i must be the New World
yes/ i'm in tune
just yes/ oh yes/ just play me
   baby/ play me/
                  yes/

From *the love space demands*

olvídalo hermana

olvídalo hermana
no le hagas ningún caso
vete vete vete vete hermana
haz lo tuyo
olvídalo

solía vivir enel mundo
deveras estar en el mundo
libre & engatusando
buenos días & gracias & linda tarde
ajá
ahora no puedo
no puedo ser amable con nadie
amable es una gran estafa
belleza común & una sonrisa en la calle
es solo una trampa

solía vivir enel mundo
una mujer enel mundo
tenía derecho al mundo
entonces me mudé a harlem
pa activar la trampa
un universo
seis cuadras de crueldad
encima de sí mismo
un túnel
que se cierra

never mind sister

never mind sister
dont pay him no mind
go go go go go go sister
do yr thing
never mind

i usedta live in the world
really be in the world
free & sweet talkin
good mornin & thank-you & nice day
uh huh
i cant now
i cant be nice to nobody
nice is such a rip-off
reglar beauty & a smile in the street
is just a set-up

i usedta be in the world
a woman in the world
i hadda right to the world
then i moved to harlem
for the set-up
a universe
six blocks of cruelty
piled up on itself
a tunnel
closin

From *for colored girls who have considered suicide/ when the rainbow is enuf*

un mito geechee de tercera generación pa tu cumple
(para John Purcell)

cuando caemos de las estrellas a las barrigas de
nuestras madres/ dicen algunos
      que hay música en el aire/ no lo crees/
nos tambaleamos por una noche
de negros/ luz grabada
            por esos hoyos negros
densidad inimaginable
resplandor inconcebible/ negro
total/ quizás el aire
en un hoyo negro/ es la quietud sagrada de los apuros en torno
al pequeño bebé moisés/ o la fuerza podría ser el fuego
que ilumina los hoyos negros/ es fiable
como el llanto de maceo/ cuando planeamos
de planeta en planeta/ oscilamos por el nuestro
hasta/ las barrigas de nuestras madres
dicen algunos
      que viene una tormenta/
& el mar azota las orillas/ como
ben webster puede irrumpir por el ojo de un huracán/
gilmore canta vapor volcánico/ bastante tonto como pa
surgir de las cenizas/ un brillo derretido
        cualquier tipo de fuego muerto
no pue'e/ volar por ninguna noche de negros/
        hasta la barriga de nuestras madres/ no pue'e llevarnos
fuera del hoyo negro/ astuto como shepp
o profético como ayler/ presión sobrecogedora
epistemológicamente/ constructos imposibles/
dejó a bird & a dapper/ fuera de kansas city
de camino a algún lugar/ debemos ir/ de camino
porque/ sí que venimos cargando estratosferas muy
de color/

a third generation geechee myth for yr birthday
(for John Purcell)

when we fall from the stars to the bellies of
our mothers/ some folks say
        they's music in the air/ dontcha think/
we tumble thru a niggah
night/ etchin light
                thru them black holes
unimaginable density
inconceivable radiance/ black
pitch/ maybe the air
in a black hole/ is the sacred hush of rushes round
lil baby moses/ or might cd be the fire
brightenin black holes/ is reliable
as maceo's wail/ when we glide
from planet to planet/ swing right past our own
down/ to our mothers' bellies
some folks say
        they's a storm a comin/
& the sea belts the shores/ how
ben webster burst thru a eye of a hurricane/
gilmore singin volcanic steam/ fool enough
to rise up from ashes/ molten glowin
                any kinda dead fire
caint/ fly out no niggah night/
        to our mothers' bellies/ caint lead us
outta black hole/ slyly shepp or
prophet ayler/ overwhelming pressure
epistemologically/ impossible constructs/
left bird & dapper lester/ outside kansas city
goin somewhere/ must be/ on our way
cuz/ we done come careenin out severely colored
stratospheres/

surgen con la fuerza de ellos/ qué soy
yo en la tradición/ & ellos no pue'en ser
no pue'en/ fumar cigarros ni hacer la luz en un hoyo blanco
tampoco/
es como tocar un tenor con una boquilla
de trompeta/ confundir a junior walker
con philip glass/ no no no/ no es nuestra costumbre
cuando/ salimos navegando de las vistas de las puntas de
las galaxias/ nos quitamos el sombrero ante marshall allen/
jimmy lyons/quizás pasa por ahí el señor coltrane/
quizás no/ podría ser un hombre banda negro itinerante y
errante
de camino a Grand Central/ pero

        tós/ venimos galopando de los cielos
de las barrigas de nuestras madres/ & la noche azul
de los negros/ tú venías recorriendo tucamino
hastaquí/ *las estrellas cayeron sobre alabama/ humor índigo*
césped nuevo/ ascensión ornitológica/ libertad ahora/
el tráfico por toda la ciudad
& *"i wonder who's lovin you"/ "better stop doggin me*
around"
"blasé"/ say hey/ *"friends and neighbors"/ "doncha*
know you make me wanna

        shout" y otras canciones volaron de la boca
          de tu madre/ saliste de su cuerpo
        & así es como/ te conviertes en
          un hombre del saxo/

surgin with the force of them/ what
am in the tradition/ & them what aint
caint/ smoke cigars or make light in a white hole
either/
be like playin a tenor wit a trumpet
mouthpiece/ mistakin junior walker
for philip glass/ no no no/ that aint our way
when/ we come sailin out the vistas of galaxies
tip/ our hats to marshall allen/
jimmy lyons/ maybe mr. coltrane gone whiz by/
maybe not/ cd be an itinerant errant one-man-negro-
band
over to Grand Central/ but
              we all/ come gallopin out the heavens
to our mothers' bellies/ & the niggah
blue night/ you was wendin yo way
down heah/ *stars fell over alabama/ mood indigo*
new grass/ ornithology/ ascension/ freedom now/
crosstown traffic
& "i wonder who's lovin you"/ "better stop doggin me
around"
"blasé"/ say hey/ "friends and neighbors"/ "doncha
know you make me wanna
        shout" flew/ out yr mother's mouth
          you/ burst out her body
        & that's how/ you come to be
          a reed man/

From *the love space demands*

vivo en la música

vivo en la música
¿es aquí donde vives?
vivo aquí en la música
vivo en la calle do ♯
mi amigo vive en la avenida si ♭
¿vives aquí en la música?
el sonido
cae en mí como la lluvia sobre otros
los saxofones me mojan la cara
fríos como el invierno en st. louis
calientes como los pimientos que paso por mis labios
pensando que son lirios
tengo 15 trompetas donde otras mujeres tienen caderas
& contrabajo pambos lados de mi corazón
camino por ahí en un piano como cualquier
otro/ caminaría porla tierra
vivo en la música
    vivo en ella
        me baño en ella
hasta la podría oler
vestir el sonido en mis dedos
el sonido cae   tan lleno de música
que podrías hacer un río donde tienes el brazo &
sostenerte
       sostenerte en una música

i live in music

i live in music
is this where you live
i live here in music
i live on c♯ street
my friend lives on b♭ avenue
do you live here in music
sound
falls round me like rain on other folks
saxophones wet my face
cold as winter in st. louis
hot like peppers i rub on my lips
thinkin they waz lilies
i got 15 trumpets where other women got hips
& a upright bass for both sides of my heart
i walk round in a piano like somebody
else/ be walkin on the earth
i live in music
   live in it
      wash in it
i cd even smell it
wear sound on my fingers
sound falls   so fulla music
ya cd make a river where yr arm is &
hold yrself
      hold yrself in a music

From *nappy edges*

los lunes hay noche latina

(para alejandro en el ribeltad)

los lunes hay noche latina
cada noche hay otro tema
el lunes hay mambo
el martes good-foot
el miércoles danza del vientre
el jueves dormir
el viernes escuchar estribillos
el sábado toca tu propia música

los lunes hay noche latina
quiero bailar bomba los miércoles
acaso me vas a arrestar
por confundir mis ritmos
podría bailar good-foot los jueves
pa compensar la pérdida de ritmo

los lunes hay noche latina
pero las trompetas & las tumbadoras son mi sangre
debo procurar un ataúd
volar desde un hidrante/ los lunes
hay noche latina
son muy estrictos/ cómo vivimos
les importa mucho/ noche latina solo los lunes
es contagioso/ peligroso
seamos nosotros mismos/ cada día

latin night is monday

(for alejandro at the ribeltad)

monday night is latin night
every night some other slot
on monday mambo
tuesday good-foot
wednesday belly-slither
thursday sleep
friday catch riffs
saturday make yr own music

monday night is latin night
i wanna bomba wednesday
are you gonna arrest me
for gettin my rhythms confused
i cd good-foot thursday
to make up for missin the beat

monday night is latin night
but trumpets & conga are my blood
i shd seek out a coffin
fly outta hydrant/ monday
night is latin night
they are very strict/ how we live
is important business/ latin night only monday
is contagious/ dangerous
let us be ourselves/ every day

From *nappy edges*

humor índigo

no siempre hasido así
ellington no era una calle
robeson no era un mero recuerdo
du bois subió las escaleras de mi padre
canturreó una melodía sobre mí
dormía en compañía de los hombres
que cambiaron el mundo

no siempre hasido así
pues ray barretto solía ser un secundario
& el pelo de dizzy no siempre fue gris
lo recuerdo   yo estaba allí
escuché en compañía de hombres
políticos tan necesarios como las coles
música hasta en los sueños

nuestra casa estaba llena de toda clase de gente
nuestras ventanas no eran de cemento o de acero
nuestras puertas se abrían como los brazos de mi papá
nos sostenía & nos amaba
niños que crecían en compañía de los hombres
viejos sureños & jóvenes acicalados
sonny til no era niño
los clovers no eran huérfanos en harapos
nuestros trovadores/ pertenecíamos al mundo entero
nkrumah no era ningún forastero
virgil aikens no era el único guerrero

no siempre hasido así
ellington no era una calle

mood indigo

it hasnt always been this way
ellington was not a street
robeson no mere memory
du bois walked up my father's stairs
hummed some tune over me
sleeping in the company of men
who changed the world

it wasnt always like this
why ray barretto used to be a side-man
& dizzy's hair was not always grey
i remember   i was there
i listened in the company of men
politics as necessary as collards
music even in our dreams

our house was filled with all kinda folks
our windows were not cement or steel
our doors opened like our daddy's arms
held us safe & loved
children growing in the company of men
old southern men & young slick ones
sonny til was not a boy
the clovers no rag-tag orphans
our crooners/ we belonged to a whole world
nkrumah was no foreigner
virgil aikens was not the only fighter

it hasnt always been this way
ellington was not a street

ii. Improvisación

𝄢 **11's**

tengo algo atascao en la garganta
es este lugar
mi bebé duerme
chequeo a ver si está viva
no sabe lo que es atragantarse
no tiene este lugar/ en la garganta
no sabe aonde estamos
cómo abrasa las membranas
se come las palabras de tu boca
te deja mamando la impotencia & el fracaso
de los contaminantes/

      toda una raza de gente nopuede hacer ná
en la disco de patinaje.

 **7/8**

tengo algo atascao en la garganta
es duro & feo/ lo vomitaría
pero lo maligno solo crece hacia
mis entrañas/ & no saldrá vivo
mi niña duerme
no sabe aonde estamos &
algún hombre/ quiere besarme las caderas
lamer el contorno de mi ombligo
ponerme las manos por tóel culo
& este lugar está en mi garganta

ii. Improvisation

 11's

there is something caught in my throat
it is this place
my baby is sleeping
i check to see if she is alive
she does not know about gagging
she does not have this place/ in her throat
she doesnt know where we are
how it sears the membranes
eats the words right outta your mouth
leaves you suckin' pollutants impotence
& failure/

      a whole race of people cant do nothin'
at the roller disco.

7/8

there is something caught in my throat
it is hard & ugly/ i wd vomit it out
but the malignancy only grows toward
my gut/ & will not come out alive
my child is sleeping
she doesnt know where we are &
some man/ wants to kiss my thighs
roll his tongue around my navel
put his hands all up my ass
& this place is in my throat

$\mathbf{9}\mathord{:}$ 5/4

    cómo le digo
  que no hay ná en mi trasero/ que
 me saque este lugar
de la garganta.
        (llegué a un lugar peligroso con un hombre que
        no estaba ahí/ porque no pue'e hacer más ná que
        hacer falsas llamadas o pedir información)

 podría decirle unas cuantas cosas
      que hay niños muertos allá fuera
      que hay mujeres desesperadas allá fuera
      que se cae el cielo
   & que me estoy ahogando
por estar donde estoy & por quienes somos.

 9/15

estamos en el siglo xx.
        (crees que la crema pa la piel artra podrá resolver
        el problema de la tez cutánea durante un conflicto nuclear
        limitado/ ¿o
acaso estás almacenando cajas de porcelana?)

 6/8

tengo esta cosa en la garganta
no puedo meterme más lenguas a la boca/
ni cigarrillos/ ni tranquilizantes/ no pue'o comer ná
debí de haberme quedao conel puto champán.
& le pedí al de la coca algo tan chévere/

𝄢 **5/4**

how can I tell him
   there is nothing up my behind/ that
  will get this place
out of my throat.
       (i went to a dangerous place with a man who
       was not there/ cuz he cant do nothin' but
       dial-a-joke or call for information)

i cd tell him a few things
    there are dead children out here
    there are desperate women out here
    the sky is falling
  & i am choking to death
cuz of where i am & who we are.

 **9/15**

this is the twentieth century.
    (do you think artra skin tone cream will solve the
    colored complexion problem during a limited nuclear
    engagement/ or
are you stocking up on porcelana?)

 **6/8**

i have this thing in my throat
i cant put no more tongues in my mouth/
no cigarettes/ no tranquilizers/ i cant eat anything
i shoulda kept my damn champagne.
& asked the coke man for something so good/

que pueda quemar este lugar
sacarlo de mi alma/ y así poder respirar
& estar pendiente de mi hija que aún duerme

 3/4

ella piensa que los unicornios & las magnolias
son cosas que se echan a la boca
aún no sabe aonde está
aún no sabe quetoloquele espera a una niña negra
es un puño en la boca o un hombre blanco
que dice que es arrogante/ porque
ella puede mirarlo alos ojos/ porque
ella no sabe aonde está.

4/4

esta cosa está en mi garganta/
& explota justo debajo de la barbilla
le dije aeste hombre quemi hija no sabía
aonde estaba/ aonde guardo a mi hija
nohay hombres blancos con pensamientos sexuales
sobre infantes/ será más lista la próxima vez
porque nova a aguantar este lugar
este gatillo fácil/ ver negros morir/ joderse
unos a otros hasta la muerte con estilo/ cuando
hay anuncios que dicen Venga & Vea a los Satin Latins/ pero tienes
    que
vestir como los dioses & las diosas blancos/
ella no vino aquí pa eso.

it would burn this place
outta my soul/ so i cd breathe
& check my daughter who is still sleeping

 3/4

she thinks unicorns & magnolias
are things to put in her mouth
she dont know where she is yet
she dont know alla black kid's gonna get
is a fist in her mouth or a white man
who says she's arrogant/ cuz
she can look him in the eye/ cuz
she dont know where she is.

4/4

this thing is in my throat/
exploding just beneath my chin
i told this man my daughter didnt know
where she was/ where i keep my child
there are no white men   with sexual thoughts
about infants/ she'll know better next time
cuz she aint having this place
this gun happy/ watch niggers die/ fuck
each other to death in style/ when
they got ads sayin' Come & See The Satin Latins/ but you gotta
dress as white gods & goddesses/
she aint here for that.

 13/15

me estoy ahogando
      (& algún hombre me miró mientras lo buscaba
      en la lluvia & me llamó luego pa decir
      que me vio en la lluvia/ buscando y no pudo
      hacer ná porque era una
      cosa estética)
tengo este lugar atascao en la garganta
me lo arrancaría & dejaría que te lo comieras
pero tengo una hija que duerme bien/ & hasta
que alguien venga a ayudarme/ tengo que seguir
tragándome este lugar/ como el resto de ustedes
orando pa que no tenga que aguantar
tó mi respeto por los seres humanos en mi puño cerrado
mi único puño de pelea/ que nos ahogaremos
eneste lugar/ & llegaremos hasta una parte
donde podamos sobrevivir.

            por favor
            no me envíen flores.
            no quiero vino blanco.
            ni siquiera quiero un techo sobre mi cabeza.
quiero sacarme este lugar dela boca
quiero que james brown deje de cantar/ que se salga pal carajo
& deje que un hombre entre

13/15

i am choking to death
        (& some man watched me looking for him
        in the rain & called me later to say
        he saw me in the rain/ looking & couldnt
        do anything about it cuz it was an
        aesthetic   thing)
this place is caught in my throat
i would tear it out & let you eat it
but i have a daughter who sleeps well/ & till
somebody comes to help me/ i'll have to keep
swallowing this place/ like the rest   of you
praying i wont have to hold
all my respect for human beings in my one closed fist
my one fistful of fight/ that we'll choke
on this place/ & make it somewhere
we could live.

        please
        dont send no flowers.
        i dont want no white wine.
        i dont even want a roof over my head.
i want this place out of my throat
i want james brown to stop singing/ to get the hell out the way
& let a man come in

From *a daughter's geography*

dama de marrón

frases oscuras de la femineidad
de nunca haber sido niña
medias notas esparcidas
sin ritmo/ sin melodía
risa distraída que cae
sobre el hombro de una niña negra
es gracioso/ es histérico
lo-sin-melodía de su baile
no le digas a nadie no le digas a ninguno
ella baila sobre latas de cerveza & tejas

esta debe ser la casa de los horrores
otra canción sin cantantes
letras/ sin voces
ni solos interrumpidos
actuaciones quenoseven

¿acaso somos demonios?
¿hijos del horror?
¿el chiste?

no le digas a nadie no le digas a ninguno
¿acaso somos animales? ¿nos hemos vuelto locos?

no puedo oír ná
sino gritos desquiciantes
& las suaves tensiones de la muerte
& me habías prometido
me habías prometido...
alguien/ que alguien
cante una canción de niña negra
que salga a la luz
pa que se conozca

lady in brown

dark phrases of womanhood
of never havin been a girl
half-notes scattered
without rhythm/ no tune
distraught laughter fallin
over a black girl's shoulder
it's funny/ it's hysterical
the melody-less-ness of her dance
don't tell nobody don't tell a soul
she's dancin on beer cans & shingles

this must be the spook house
another song with no singers
lyrics/ no voices
& interrupted solos
unseen performances

are we ghouls?
children of horror?
the joke?

don't tell nobody don't tell a soul
are we animals? have we gone crazy?

i can't hear anythin
but maddening screams
& the soft strains of death
& you promised me
you promised me . . .
somebody/ anybody
sing a black girl's song
bring her out
to know herself

pa que te conozca
pero canta sus ritmos
cariño/ lucha/ tiempos duros
canta la canción de su vida
ha estado muerta por tanto tiempo
encerrada en el silencio por tanto tiempo
no reconoce el sonido
de su propia voz
su belleza infinita
es notas blancas esparcidas
sin ritmo/ sin melodía
cántale sus suspiros
cántale la canción de sus posibilidades
cántale un góspel justo
que nazca
que nazca
& que la traten con calidez.

estoy en las afueras de chicago
estoy en las afueras de detroit
estoy en las afueras de houston
estoy en las afueras de baltimore
estoy en las afueras de san francisco
estoy en las afueras de manhattan
estoy en las afueras de st. louis

& esto es pa las chicas de color que han considerado el suicidio
pero se han movido al final de sus propios arco iris.

to know you
but sing her rhythms
carin/ struggle/ hard times
sing her song of life
she's been dead so long
closed in silence so long
she doesn't know the sound
of her own voice
her infinite beauty
she's half-notes scattered
without rhythm/ no tune
sing her sighs
sing the song of her possibilities
sing a righteous gospel
let her be born
let her be born
& handled warmly.

i'm outside chicago
i'm outside detroit
i'm outside houston
i'm outside baltimore
i'm outside san francisco
i'm outside manhattan
i'm outside st. louis

& this is for colored girls who have considered suicide
but moved to the end of their own rainbows.

From *for colored girls who have considered suicide/ when the rainbow
is enuf*

18 de marzo de 1984

oscilan hombres de musgo español
machetes en mano
cortan la caña los pinos & cipreses
retoman el suelo que es nuestro
el algodón rojo de sangre
el arroz que nos pudre las piernas

oscilan hombres de musgo español
cuelgan lánguidos de esas cuerdas de linchamiento
¿aire / dónde está el aire?
respiramos nuestras muertes con tanta casualidad
como colar el café de la mañana
el olor tan familiar el tufillo
nos lleva escaleras abajo a toda prisa
donde los fantasmas pisan en una sola fila
sobre nuestros cuerpos
a la espera de que podamos ver algo

oscilan hombres de musgo español mientras
recopilo mis pequeñas pertenencias/ mi pasado
me deja demorarme solo un poquito más
antes de que me una a ustedes en una sola fila
pisando sobre nuestros parientes de sangre
que aún coquetean con la muerte
que confunden a al johnson con dr. j
déjenme caminar con ustedes un rato más
estoy aprendiendo a usar el machete
en el salvador usamos fusiles galil
libramos la guerra con la muerte
florecemos a pesar de las torturas
no siempre basta con machetes//

18 march 1984

swing spanish moss men
machetes in hand
cut back the cane the pines & cypress
take back the soil that is our own
the cotton red with blood
rice rotting our legs away

swing spanish moss men
hang languid from those lynching ropes
air / where is there air?
we breathe our deaths so casually
like making morning coffee
the smell so familiar whiffs of it
bring us running downstairs
where ghosts step in single file
over our bodies
hoping we might see anything

swing spanish moss men while I
gather my small parcels/my past
let me tarry on just a little further
before I join you in single filo
stepping over our blood kin
still flirting with death
mistaking al jolson for dr. j
let me walk with you just a bit longer
i'm learning to use my machete
in el salvador we use galil machine guns
wage war on death
blossoming despite the tortures
machetes are not always enough //

From *ridin' the moon in texas*

roble vivo

no hay indicadores
solo aquel roble fornido que se iza
hasta las nubes
imagino
que había un bosque antes y
animales salvajes y libres   olisquean pastan
se aprovechan de la sombra de este árbol colosal
alguna vez quizás los niños jugaron alrededor del tronco
algún niño valiente intentó trepar las ramas azotadas
por el viento / alguna vez amantes habrán comido
cerca de la base
solos junto a la autopista, aunque
conozco cinco personas de color que colgaron
de él/ cinco personas de color al mismo tiempo
no es como si alguno dellos adornara las ramas del roble
y luego otro más
en otro día.
a tós los ahorcaron a la vez.
cuatro hombres y una mujer preñada
pendían y se sacudían sin aliento
bajo las cuerdas hasta morir
este es un árbol que tós
conocen/ cinco negros colgados
y ya está/ no hubo arrestos/
ni demostraciones solo el silencio denso
del miedo y el odio/ sin otro indicador que la neblina nocturna.

live oak

no markers
only that burly oak reaching
towards the clouds
I imagine
there was a forest once and
wild free animals   nuzzling grazing
taking in the shade of that gargantuan tree
once children maybe played round the trunk
some brave boy tried to climb the windswept
branches / once lovers maybe picnicked
by its base
alone by the highway, though
I know five colored people were hanged
from it/ five colored people all at the same time
not like one of 'em graced the limbs of the oak
and then another
on some other day.
they were all hanged at once.
four men and one pregnant woman
dangled breathless and jerking
neath the ropes til they died
this is a tree everybody
knows about/ five niggahs strung up
and that was that/ no arrests/
no demonstrations just the heavy silence
of fear and hate / no markers but the night mists.

caja & poste

debemos fabricar tótems
de qué otra forma nos sentirán los espíritus
de qué otra forma sabrán que debemos alcanzarlos
dentro de nosotros mismos / nuestros espíritus
rondan los cielos la tierra & los mares
tal y como otras deidades / requerimos
honores sacrificios & ofrendas
aquellas cosas que debemos darnos a nosotros mismos
los aztecas vestían las pieles de los muertos
los yoruba regalan flores blancas a yemayá
& champán / los incas ofrecían oro
y hojas de coca / tenemos que construir tótems
pa los espíritus / debemos adorarnos a nosotros mismos
que no se pueda profanar la tierra
con nuestro desdén / nuestra ignorancia del ritual
después de tó el universo nos ha dado
las estaciones / el calor de amar.

box & pole

we must make totems
how else can the spirits feel us
how else can they know we must reach
for them in ourselves / our spirits
roam the skies the soil & the seas
not unlike other deities / we require
homage sacrifice & offerings
those things we must give ourselves
aztecs dressed in the skins of the dead
yorubans deliver yemaya white blossoms
& champagne / incas offered gold
& coca leaves / we must build totems
for the spirits / we must worship ourselves
that the earth not be defiled
by our neglect / our ignorance of ritual
after all the universe has given us
the seasons / the warmth of loving.

From *ridin' the moon in texas*

manos & agarrar

1)

manos & agarrar
lenguas & clítoris
se combinan muy bien
la forma en que
el sol besa el océano al amanecer
has caído
desde el interior
de tumbadoras que ríen
te oigo reír
en el túnel
resbalón danzante de mujer
desdelas ramas del árbol
sus caderas están alegres
de verte

2)

en la noche/ las velas de ochún
hacen olas de brillo etéreo
por los vellos de tu vientre
he hablado con las estrellas
limitadas a hoyos negros
de la vía láctea
quieren caer alrededor tuyo
me envidian las mujeres
hasta más brillantes que el sol

3)

estabas acurrucado
bajo la ventana
como gatitos en las tetas de mykko
algunos visitantes

hands & holding

1)

hands & holding
tongues & clit
go well together
the way
the sun kisses the ocean at dawn
you have fallen
from the inside
of laughin congas
i hear you smilin
in the tunnel
women glissade
from tree limbs
their hips are so glad
to see you

2)

in the night/ ochun's candles
make ether-glow waves
thru the hairs on yr stomach
i have spoken to stars
confined to black holes
from the milky way
they want to fall round you
i am envied by ladies
brighter even than the sun

3)

you were curled
under the window
like kittens at mykko's tits
some visitors

te llevaron a un arco iris verdadero
dormiste
ojos amplios agua suave
digo al final del arco iris
cocinando gumbo en una olla de oro

4)
una mujer de trinidad
me dice que un hombre-de-sangre-caliente
baila como los vientos mansos
en las galerías haitianas/
tu tacto es firme
como las raíces a la tierra

5)
no puedo hablar
tus ojos me han
robado la lengua
ahora solo sabe
moverse de tus labios
a tu cadera

took you towards the true rainbow
you slept
eyes wide water soft
i sit at the end of the rainbow
makin gumbo in a pot of gold

4)

a trinidadian woman
tells me a hot-blooded man
dances like slow winds
in haitian halls/
yr touch is firm
like roots to soil

5)

i cannot speak
yr eyes have
stolen my tongue
only knows
to move from yr lips
to yr thigh

From *nappy edges*

baile tropical
(para mercedes baptista)

en bahía las mujeres envuelven
la ropa como girasoles
en sus cabezas se mueven
como olas costeras suaves en
ráfagas violetas & onduladas
    la samba
riza cada músculo
tiembla se levanta a ritmos
baila coquetea
aretes de coral rosado implacables
que provocan a la altura de los hombros
mover una mano es el secreto
de medianoche dentro-fuera
se ríen las caderas ajajajaja
tobillos boyantes guían los dedos
que amasan la tierra hasta achicarla
las preciosas calles marrones
los cuerpos cantan plata
tintinean los brazaletes
en bahía las mujeres se mueven
con gracia aún se mecen
aún se mecen altas y graciosas
sus miembros son cascadas
aún brotan como flores graciosas
ritmos intricados de atardeceres
nubes que se mecen graciosas aún
se mecen abrazando los cielos
en bahía
    las mujeres
        samban

tropical dance

(for mercedes baptista)

en bahia women wrap
cloth like sun flowers
round their heads move
like soft coast waves in
velvet rufflin gusts of
wind
    the samba
ripples every muscle
quivers wakes up to rhythms
dances flirts
mercilessly pink coral earrings
taunt at shoulder's length
one hand motion is the midnight
secret in-out in-out in-out
hips laugh uhuhuh
ankles-buoyant guide toes
kneadin the earth small
winsome streets brown
bodies sing silver
bracelets tinklin
en bahia women move
graciously still swayin
still tall swayin graciously
ripplin the samba swayin
limbs like water-falls
still gracious flowers burst
intricate rhythms of sunsets
swayin clouds gracious still
sway embracin the skies
en bahia
  women
    samba

From *nappy edges*

amarte es un éxtasis para mí

creo que vi una bandada de flamencos que meditaba
ahí alante del almacén de muebles bekin's/
pero ehtaba equivocá/
los pavos reales se han recluido por los muelles cantando fados
y fruncen las plumas que el ego les ha dado en abundancia/
tomo la mano de tó el mundo/
los cuerpos de alguna gente son sudor pa mí/
mguanda mwile tarabu mikey mr. nim/
m/ sieur henri
serenatas de mujeres honky tonk en nashira's kitchen/
Bárbara la reprochada sirve flores de lirio jengibre fresco
nudo negro   & un brebaje con especias en platos de aluminio/
ifá se manifiesta en las verduras furtivas
& lo azul de sus ojos flota
alrededor de mi corazón/
vinos de zarzamora albaricoque manzanas orgánicas
rebotan en mi corazón/
la emperatriz machaca opio sobrela estufa/
las articulaciones parecen pegadas al dedo índice del taxi/
norman   no trajo sus tambores/
kapuenda está bordada de cornalinas
njeri es lavanda

lovin you is ecstasy to me

i thought i saw a flock of flamingoes meditatin
cross dere from de bekin's furniture warehouse/
bt i waz mistaken/
peacocks have sequestered themselves by the docks singin dirges
n ruffling feathers ego had too abundantly supplied/
i hold everybody's hand/
some people's bodies are sweat next to me/
mguanda mwile tarabu mikey mr. nim/
m/sieur henri
serenades the honkytonk woman in nashira's kitchen/
barretted barbara serves lily flowers pickled ginger
blk tree fungus   & spiced broth in aluminum plates/
ifa is manifest in furtive greens
& the blueness of her eyes floats
round my heart/
wines of blkberry apricot organic apples
bounce in my heart/
the empress singes opium over de stove/
joints seem taped to taxi's index finger/
norman   didn't bring his drums/
javier is embroidered with cornelians
njeri is lavender

From *nappy edges*

entre una bailarina & un poeta
(para conyus)

oscilaba desde la barra   firme   en control
le dolían las piernas, implacables   hasta rio
mientras él apuntaba
         'quiero amarte   como bailo yo
           cuando sufro   estoy mejorando'
el poeta firmó su nombre en líneas que eclipsan la realidá
no podía recuperar el aliento   el lenguaje era
sobrecogedor
         'puedo amar lo que entiendo
           cuando no entiendo   adoro'
se puso el lápiz en el bolsillo & se sentó
en medio de un círculo caprichoso
ella tiró un plié   se contrajo   sudó
& creció su confianza en la contienda
pa superar la forma   apenas trascender pantorrillas tobillos
   caderas
pertrechos   como una banda musical

el baile es del espíritu   el cuerpo   su sacrificio
pa bailar
      & brincó ante el poeta
saltó
tiró un chasé   ante el poeta   atinó
el aire era un amante insolente   &   la bailarina
era justa elegida pa conquistar el espacio

jadeó   sudó   & su leotardo olía a calor
& a mujer   & se rio
mientras el poeta se acariciaba la mejilla
ella se deslizó alrededor de él   su cuerpo   giraba como una
   cobra-viento
& ella encontró el alma del poeta   en el espacio

between a dancer & a poet

(for conyus)

she swayed from the barre   taut   in control
her legs hurt mercilessly   she even laughed
while he took notes
      'i wanna love you   like i dance
         when i hurt   i'm gettin better'
the poet signed his name to lines eclipsin reality
he cdnt catch his breath   the language waz
overpowerin
      'i can love what i understand
        when i dont understand   i worship'
he put his pencil in his pocket & sat
      in the middle of a whimsical circle
the dancer pliéed   she contracted   she sweat
& grew confident in her struggle
to surpass form   transcend calves ankles hips merely
accoutrements   like a music stand

dance is of the spirit   the body   her sacrifice
to dance
      & she pranced before the poet
leaped
chasséd   before the poet   she struck
the air waz an impudent lover   &   the dancer
was righteous chosen to conquer space

she panted   she sweat   & her leotard smelled of heat
& woman   & she laughed
while the poet fondled his own cheek
she slid round him   her body   swirled like a cobra-wind
& she located the poet's soul   in space

él perdió el espíritu   en la ráfaga
de la valentía de ella   & ella gritó
        'quiero amarte como bailo yo
            salvaje & delicada   alcanzando lo que no conozco
                quiero amarte alrededor de tu cuerpo
                    dentro-fuera-de-él   sin suelo sin piso

                quiero amarte donde pueda bailar'
& ella acariciaba el aire como un helecho de mar
            quemándose en el foso de girasoles antiguos
        cargando el alma del poeta en un rubor de las mejillas
el corazón de él flotaba   en el sudor de ella

            he lost his spirit   in the rush
of her darin   & she screamed
         'i wanna love you like i dance
            wild & delicate   reachin for what i do not know
                i wanna love you all round yr body
                    in-out-of-it   no grounds no floor

            i wanna love you where i can dance'
& she caressed the air like an ocean fern
         blazin in the pits of ancient sunflowers
     carryin the poet's soul in the blush of her cheeks
his heart lingerin   in her sweat

From *nappy edges*

111

nupcias de nueva orleans

sabía que conocería los confines de la tierra
     antes dequeme tomaras completa
rondaría chichén itzá en una picop/
     da tres pasos/ tres revoloteos/ tres palmadas
revoloteo ku-dapi chasé/ assemblé
alas de una polilla imperial aletean en tu lengua

tú/
no podías tomarme de otra manera/ que no fuera
de cantazo
el sol nunca se pone/ yazco desnuda
al amanecer/ al atardecer
de un blues desnudo de nuez moscada a un *soleil* tentador y jadeante
rociando/ desiertos resonantes
por mis caderas mis pechos mi corazón
deseando labios que no estén familiarizados con otros labios
allá abajo que no sean los míos

todas las frutas arrancadas arriba/ abajo & más allá
la circunferencia de la tierra/ ahora yo
el ecuador debe estar ahora en mi cintura/ esconde la inocencia
entre las nubes/ las nieves del monte mckinley
me limpian/ endurecen/ adormecen las memorias
de otros que no son yo

en el círculo de baños termales revivo
salto salvaje alrededor de tus bigotes/ me libero
alazana caprichosa luchando con el bocado/ de tu
    predilección
tendrás que tomarme de esta manera
marcada & apache en cuero blanco por *la coupole*

leo vorazmente sobre hombres/ que viajan de mujer en mujer
no de milla en milla/ de amor en amor

112

new orleans nuptials

i knew i'd know the ends of the earth
          before you'd have me fully
i'd prowl chichén itzá in a pick-up truck/
          take three steps/ three flaps/ three slaps
ku-dapi flap chassé/ assemblée
wings of an imperial moth fluttering over your tongue

you/
you could have me no other way/ than
all at once
the sun never sets/ i lay naked
at dawn/ at dusk
a nutmeg nude blues to a heaving tempting *soleil*
spraying/ blaring deserts
cross my thighs my breast my heart
longing for lips no longer familiar with other labia
than mine

all fruits plucked above/ below & around
the circumference of the earth/ now me
the equator must now be my waist/ hiding innocence
among clouds/ the snows of mt. mckinley
cleansing me/ hardening/ making numb memories
of any other than me

at the circle hot springs i come alive
leap wildly round your whiskers/ breaking away
skittish sorrel wrestling with the bit/ of your choosing
you'd have to have me this way
brandied & apache in white leather by *la coupole*

i read voraciously of men/ who travel woman to woman
not mile by mile/ love by love

hombres que se enredan tanto con los olores/
cualesquiera que les presentemos/
mentones lapislázuli arcilla en polvo mármol pulido bosque de
pino cerezo en cera losas de formas arbitrarias pintadas a mano/
extremidades hexagonales te rodean el pecho/ espirales de dedos
te soban el cuello/ déjame disfrutar a medianoche bajo el sol
tan suave me tomas casi completa en el destello
      del abedul
los álamos crujen como si respirara
otra cosa que no fuera tó/ (tengo que averiguar tercios mitades
        cuartos octavos dieciseisavos onceavos
            treceavos/
todas las posibilidades de división)

sabría que conocería los confines de la tierra
      antes dequeme tomaras por completo
por encima de tó/ por encima de las montañas
rosas de coral florecen desde las esquinas de mi boca/
los salmones avanzan feroces/ se lanzan por el arco
      de nuestros vientres
más torrentes de agua clara se cuelan por nuestras caderas/
mis pantorrillas buscan arroyos corrientes ensenadas de ti
      pa cubrirme
tortillas azules se imaginan como placenta/ una & otra vez
crezco/ mi cabello sigue a los horizontes
talla mis visiones como caoba bambú cedro/ madejas
de piel de oveja musgo jalapeños arropan mis sienes
de los confines de la tierra he regresado pa tenerte
y nunca nadie me había tenido/

habla cualquier lengua/ sabré lo que dices
mira a cualquier parte/ veré lo que ves
sostenme/ déjame besarte
ahora/ nos acercamos al cielo

114

men who so entangle themselves with smells/
however we present ourselves/
lapis chins dusted clay polished marble beaten brush waxed
cherrywood hand painted tiles of arbitrary shapes/
hexagonal limbs wound round your chest/ spirals of fingers
rubbing your neck/ let me bask at midnight in sunlight
so slick you take me almost wholly in the glimmer
    of the birch
cottonwoods rustle like i am breathing
no other way than all/ (i must ferret out triplets halves
        quarters eighths sixteenths elevenths
            thirteenths/
any possibilities of divisions)

i knew i'd know the ends of the earth
    before you'd have me fully
above all/ above the mountains
coral roses bloom from the corners of my mouth/
salmon rush ferociously/ throwin themselves thru the arc
    of our bellies
more rushes of clear waters seep tween our thighs/
my calves search out brooks streams coves of you
    to swathe me
blue tortillas imagine themselves placenta/ over & over
i am growing/ my hair follows the horizons
carving my visions like mahogany bamboo cedar/ skeins
of sheepskin moss jalapeñas envelop my temples
from the ends of the earth i've come back to have you
as no one has had me before/

speak any language/ i'll know what you mean
look somewhere/ i'll see what you see
hold me/ let me kiss you
now/ we approach heaven

From *ridin' the moon in texas*

inconteniblemente bronce, bello & mío

i.

toda la vida han estado cerca de mí
estos hombres/
    algunos por algún tiempo como el
amigo de mi padre que manejaba
cada verano desde denver hasta
st. louis/ con alguna mujer
blanca distinta/ recuerdo que a una
le caía bien/ tenía el pelo rubio rosado
me preguntaba/ por qué te caigo bien
estás con él & él es mío
es de color/ siempre lo será
así/ como yo/ pienso
que él conocía que mi preciosa
alma de ocho años anhelaba
hace rato llegar con uno/
uno de esos hombres de color
que fuera mío/ a propósito/ no
solo a causa de algún problema de
pigmentación/ o alguna cláusula de derechos
adquiridos de misisipi/ he vivido cerca
del agua/ del río/ el cieno
me sancochaba las pantorrillas/ me reía con
los chamaquitos/ los niños que serían
hombres negros algún día
    si pudieran vivir tanto tiempo

me trajo rocas/ cada viaje
cuarzo mármol granito & arenisca
óvalos de ónix que podía guardar pa mí cuando
se iba en el carro con la mujer blanca
nunca me puse triste/ no sabía que podía

irrepressibly bronze, beautiful & mine

i.

all my life they've been near me
these men/
     some for a while like the
friend of my father's who drove
each summer from denver to
st. louis/ with some different
white woman/ i remember one seemed
to like me/ she had rose blond hair
i wondered/ why do you like me
you're with him & he's mine
he's colored/ he'll always be
like that/ like me/ i think
he knew my eight-year-old
precocious soul was hankering
for days to come with one/
one of them colored fellas
who'd be mine/ on purpose/ not
just cause of some pigmentation
problem/ or a grandfather clause
in mississpippi/ i lived there near
the water/ the river/ the silt
caking my calves/ me laughin with
the younguns/ the boys who'd be
black men one day
     if they lived so long

he brought me rocks/ each sojourn
quartz marble granite & sandstone
onyx ovals i could hold onto when
he drove off with the white woman
i never felt sad/ i didn't know i might

estar experimentando el rechazo/ una niñita
de color con una piedra de ébano
en la palma de la mano
sabía que ese era su corazón
aónde podría ir un hombre sin su corazón
una niña por el misisipi agarrando
sueños/ pero aferrarse a un hombre
solo de noche & motown me sacó a bailar
me cantó dulces corrientes de sudor
besos húmedos/ aquellos torsos arrogantes
que retaban a los blanquitos o a los tontos a
que mirarnos mal/ no solo mirarnos
de forma rara & tó se acabaría
o apenas comenzaría

mírame maldito negro hermoso

echa pacá/ he crecido
ahora & las piedras no se quedan
quietas en mi mano/ sabes
cómo erupcionan los volcanes negros
dicen que cuando miles davis logra
un suspiro/ dicen que erupcionan
cuando los blackstone rangers
salen a pasear/ los volcanes negros filtran
lava donde quiera que haya amor verdadero
no hablo ahora de
un grito y un jadeo o un baile por un peso
pero cuando hay amor de verdá
los volcanes rezuman lava
& siempre ha sido mía
siempre mi amor como la Biblia
dice ojo por ojo/ hay
un yo pa un tú

be experiencing rejection/ a little
colored girl with an ebony stone
in the palm of her hand
i knew that was his heart
where could a man go without his heart
a child by the mississippi grasping
dreams/ yet to grab holto a man
but nighttime & motown asked me to dance
sang sweet streams of sweat
moist kisses/ those arrogant torsos
daring crackers or a fool to
look the wrong way/ no just look
a funny way & it'd be over
or just begun

look at me pretty niggah

bring it over here/ i'm grown
now & the stones don't sit
static in my hand/ you know
how it is black volcanoes erupt
they say when miles davis manages
to whisper/ they erupt they say
when the blackstone rangers take
a stroll/ black volcanoes seep
lava anywhere there's true love
now i'm not talkin about
a hoot and holler or a dance on a dime
but whenever there's true
love/ black volcanoes seep lava
& it's always been mine
always my dear like the Bible
says an eye for an eye/ there's
a me for a you

echa pacá cariño
te he guardado el corazón
en mi mano desde niña
a veces he estado preocupada
        pero he tenido que crecer también
porque quería tó lo que eras
tó lo que eres/ ahora eres un hombre
tienes al mundo mirando cada paso
que das/ tengo tu corazón
& por el misisipi/ cuando era una
        niña/ llamábamos a eso un ritmo
mi dulce frijol pinto
cascarilla bañada en miel

        echa pacá/ no tengo miedo

te conozco de toda la vida

        & esto cariño es solo el
principio
el primer atisbo de lo que van a escuchar
no hay ninguna mentira que no podamos cantar
no te abochornes/ solo aparece
aquí mismo
        como te tengo/ aquellas
veces en que eres marrón y húmedo/ aquellas
veces que tu fuerza no tiene par alguno
solo sé
        &
recuérdame/ ay allá cuando
te montaste en el carro & huiste
        tu corazón en la palma
                de mi mano niña

bring it on baby
i've been holding your heart in
my hand since i was a child
i've been preoccupied on occasion
    but i had to grow some too
cause i wanted what all you were
what all you are/ now you're a man
you've got the world watchin your
every move/ i've got your heart
& by the mississippi/ when i was a
    child/ we callt that a groove
sweet black-eyed pea
honey-dripped husk

    bring it on/ i'm not afraid

i've known you all my life

    & this my dear is just the
beginning
the first inkling of what they're gonna
    hear
it ain't no lie that we could sing
don't be embarassed/ just appear
right there
    the way i have you/ those
times you're brown & wet/ those
times your strength can't be met
just be
    &
remember me/ oh back then
when you rode off & left
    your heart in the palm
        of my child hand

ii.

entre palmas lagartijos que silban
anidan por las raíces recién húmedas
raíces por las pencas de palma el sol
deleita a los amantes los invita
a que rápido hagan el amor entre
arenas húmedas que rezuman por los pies
bájate el pecho las piernas enjutas
& gruesas el pelo suelto hasta abajo
enaguas/ pantis de encaje
labios perfumados que saltan sobre
hombros músculos tocan música
donde solo había acacias & macacos
solo atrevido/ muchos dúos
han sido abandonados por los troncos
de palma en busca de
la luz de la luna/ avanzan al cielo
mientras las lenguas se
entrelazan/ rocío como miel
que se les escurre de los labios
tós los cielos caídos por
sus pies/

      los jaguares acechan cuando sus
ojos se encuentran.

ii.

among palms whistling lizards
nestle by roots freshly humid
roots by palm fronds the sun
tickles lovers inviting them to
make quickly some love in
moist sands seeping through toes
pull down the bosom the legs
wiry & thick haired pull down
the petticoats/ lace panties
perfumed lips skipping over
shoulders muscles making music
where before only acacias & macaws
dared solo/ many duets
have been abandoned by the trunks
of palms searching for
moonlight/ rushing toward the sky
as tongues would wrap round
each other/ dew like honey
slipping from their lips
whole skies fallen by
their feet/

        jaguars prowl when their
eyes meet.

From *the love space demands*

"si ando el camino sin ti, ¿adónde voy?"
—*los Isley Brothers*

ahí/ a la derecha de venus
                cerca de donde tu león
acecha nuestro horizonte/   mira/
escucha/
brilla escarlata/ arde-escarlata/ aplaca mi corazón
ahí/   cerca de ti/ *amarillo* candente/
ay/ diría/ mi nuevo día
                mi amanecer/
tusdedos trazan la ráfaga de mis labios/
        siempre tan reverentes/
          siempre tan hambrientos/

aquí/
a la derecha de venus/
              mi lengua/
           relámpago tropical/
ráfaga/ ahora/ suave/ entre mis dedos/ los mares menguan
& en esta arena/ estoy de vuelta
        marejada impredecible
un lirio de agua dulce/ en el atlántico norte/
cuando me tocas/   sí
así es como las perlas/ se arrancan desde la blancura de mis
huesos
      a la punta de tusdedos/
        chicago dura indiscutible
          consecuencias rococó/
& esto/ el delta del misisipi/ entre mis caderas
tusegundo toque/ prohíbe
algo menor/ que la fluidez primordial/
no/
acostada junto a ti/
        la contracorriente en carmel/

"if i go all the way without you where would i go?"
—*The Isley Brothers*

there/ to the right of venus
               close to where yr lion
stalks our horizon/   see/
listen/
glow scarlet/ char-scarlet/ set my heart down
there/   near you/ scaldin *amarillo*/
oh/ say/ my new day
               my dawn/
yr fingers trace the rush of my lips/
        ever so reverent/
        ever so hungry/

here/
to the right side of venus/
               my tongue/
               tropical lightenin/
rush/ now/ softly/ tween my toes/ the seas ebb
& in these sands/ i've come back/
        an unpredictable swell
a fresh water lily/ in the north atlantic/
when you touch me/   yes
that's how pearls somehow/ rip from the white of my
bones
   to yr fingertips/
      incontrovertible hard chicago
        rococo implications/
& this/ the mississippi delta/ tween my thighs
yr second touch/ forbids
a thing less/ than primordial fluidity/
no/
i lay next to you/
      the undertow at carmel/

el río ruso/ toca los tallos de lo mejor/ de
humboldt county
& maldita sea/
       ¿qué te hace pensar/ que mi espina dorsal es
tu falla de san andrés/
personal?

         retumbándose/los campos serenos dan paso a la
  lluvia/
hastaque
me abro/ humedá profunda trigueña & negra
       cobalto quebrilla en todas partes/
estamos
ahí/
       donde el pacífico acaricia mis más alejadas
costas/ detroit-alta-ocre/ cerca delas secoyas/
      voy trepando
        me persigues/ rama por rama/
         arrancando las estrellas coloridas/ dela
noche
       las deslizas/ sobre milengua/
&
pensé quepodía superar/
los peligros/ devivir
   en la cuenca del pacífico/
cuando te miro/
yo
sé/ que me juego la vida/
  arrojo la rázon/ al interior remoto de los far
rockaways/
    yendo/ abandonándolo/ tó/ sin
protesta/
abandonando/ episodios meteorológicos

the russian river/ feelin up stalks of the best/ of
humboldt county
& damn it/
                  what makes you think/ my spine is
yr personal/
san andreas fault?

                  shiftin/ serene fields break for rain/
til
i open/ deep brown moist & black
                  cobalt sparklin everywhere/
we are
there/
                  where the pacific fondles my furthest
shores/ detroit-high-russet/ near redwoods/
                  i am climbin
                        you chase me/ from limb to limb/
                              pullin the colored stars/ out the
night
                        slippin em/ over my tongue/
&
i thought i cd get over/
the dangers/ of livin
        on the pacific rim/
when i look at you/
i
know/ i am riskin my life/
      tossin reason/ to the outback of the far
rockaways/
        goin/ givin up/ everything/ with out
protest/
givin up/ meterological episodes

los montes apalaches/
                entregando/ islas del estrecho
de puget/
                travis county zona montañosa/
regalando/ tesoros/
que
nunca
reclamé/
        hasta que te conocí/

mi propio atardecer de diciembre/ cipreses burlones/
hasta los *bikers* dela calle campbell/ en el centro de oakland
dejé decombatir/
lo que no/ sea ordenado/ imaginado/ legítimo
sí/ sí
abrázame
como/ la noche arropa a wyoming/
& soy más/ de lo que no soy/
podría cantar letras sacras/ pa canciones que no me sé/
mi mejilla/ roza los cactus negros/ y encaracolados detu
pecho/
& soy inundación de supernovas/
si me besas así/ soy pantano moreno
tuslabios/ invitan a la luna/ a divagar/
nuestras bocas se abren & cantan/
sí/
nuestras lenguas/
el filo de la tierra/

the appalachian mountains/
                    handin over/ islands from puget
sound/
                    travis county hill country/
givin away/ treasures/
i
never
claimed/
         til i felt you/

my own december sunset/ teasin cypress/
even campbell street bikers/ in downtown oakland/
i stopped resistin/
what won't/ be orderly/ imagined/ legitimate/
yes/ yes/
hold me
like/ the night grabs wyoming/
& i am more/ than i am not/
i cd sing sacred lyrics/ to songs i don't know/
my cheek/ rubs gainst the nappy black/ cacti of yr
chest/
& i am a flood of supernovas/
if you kiss me like that/ i'm browned wetlands
yr lips/ invite the moon/ to meander/
our mouths open & sing/
yes/
our tongues/
the edge of the earth/

From *the love space demands*

se alzan los guerreros caídos

he estado casada con bob marley
por lo menos 17 años
pero solía llamarlo smokey robinson
es difícil recordar que yo
era menor cuando nos casamos &
me cambié la fecha de nacimiento
tantas veces queno puedo contar los años
solo las satisfacciones

bob marley es mi marido
de que nuestra unión sea legal tiene que ver
con aonde vivas & si tienes buena opinión
sobre halie selassie/ el león de judá
mis hijos se esconden enel bosque delos tucanes
se columpian de sus rastas rojas/ trepan
jims de la jungla de lapislázuli bajo el cuidado
de los buenos hombres de color de urano/
donde tós los hombres de color son maestros preescolares/
donde cantan las canciones de mi marido
donde nos exodeamos fuera de aquí
donde las místicas naturales
se *jammean* tó el tiempo &
cae lluvia de alegría en casa de tóel mundo

no te miento no
bob marley me mantiene
porque quiere darme algo de amor
lleva tocando mipuerta tres años
& aún está ahí de seguro
brinca
grita
sacude la cabeza

rise up fallen fighters

i've been married to bob marley
for at least 17 years
but i usedta call him smokey robinson
it's hard to remember i
waz underage at the time of our union &
changed my birthdate
so much i cant count the years
only the satisfaction

bob marley is my husband
whether our marriage is legal has to do
with where you live & if you think highly
of haile selassie/ the lion of judah
my children are hiding in toco forest
they swing on their rasta red hair/ climbin
jungle jims of lapis under the supervision
of the good colored men from uranus/
where all colored men are kindergarten teachers/
where they sing my husband's songs
where we exodus-ed outta here
where natural mystics
be jammin alla time &
they be raining joy on everybody house

i tell you no lie
bob marley take care of me
cuz he wanna give me some love
been knockin on my door three year
& he still here for sure
he jump
he scream
he shake he head

cierra el ojo
va a la tierra prometida
espera por mí en la estrella
arde
canta
quiere *jammear* conmigo &
no espera en vano
está en el movimiento del pueblo
brinca
grita
cierra el ojo
gira su cabeza de londres a canal street
se le cae una trenza del sol
me ve
pone su marca aquí
yo alcanzo el mundo
él me lo dio
trabajo   descanso   lo amo en el aire
podría acariciar el cielo
ver a kingston eclipsar la culpa
en el nombre del señor
el león de judá

los guerreros de david
arriba arriba guerreros caídos
muéstrenme la tierra prometida
muéstrenme el universo
la tierra de nuestros padres
rebélense
anuncien la venida del reino de los herederos legítimos
trepo hasta la luna por la vía rasta
las tierras de nuestros padres
rebelándose

he close he eye
he be in the promised land
he wait for me on star
he blaze
he sing
he wanna jam it wit me &
he dont wait in vain
he in the movement of the people
he jump
he scream
he shake he head
he close he eye
he head twirl from london to canal street
he braid fall from the sun
he see me
he lay his mark here
i reach for the world
he give it to me
i work   i rest   i love him in the air
i cd fondle the sky
watch kingston eclipse guiltiness
in the name of the lord
the lion of judah

david's warriors
rise up rise up fallen fighters
show me the promised land
show me round the universe
our fathers' land
rise up
announce the comin of the kingdom rightful heir
i climbin to the moon on the rasta-thruway
our father land
risin up

la tierra hasta canta & brinca
el cielo quiere *jammear* tó el día
las estrellas olvidan su debilidad
& bailan
arriba guerreros caídos
liberen las estrellas
bailen con el universo
& háganlo nuestro

ay háganlo/ háganlo nuestro
ay háganlo/ háganlo nuestro

the land even sing & jump
the sky want to jam all thru the day
the stars forget they weakness
& dance
rise up fallen fighters
unfetter the stars
dance with the universe
& make it ours

oh, make it/ make it ours
oh make it/ make it ours.

From *from okra to greens*

elegancia al extremo
(para cecil taylor)

elegancia al extremo
da estilo a las horas
de sonsacar el calor de
ninguna parte

barriobajeros elegantes
intelectuales elegantes
ornitólogos elegantes
botánicos elegantes

pero la elegancia al extremo ayuda más
al extraño que titubea
en dar lo que hay
por miedo a desatar la locura
que   está a veces
separada de las costumbres contemporáneas
de realidades arquetípicas o de la gracia

en la ausencia de elegancia extrema
la locura puede acomodarse como
un gauloises que quema seda japonesa
a pesar de su gran sofisticación
hasta la seda debe preguntar
cómo se consume tan discretamente

elegance in the extreme
(for cecil taylor)

elegance in the extreme
gives style to the hours
of coaxing warmth outta
no where

elegant hoodlums
elegant intellectuals
elegant ornithologists
elegant botanists

but elegance in the extreme helps most
the stranger who hesitates
to give what there is
for fear of unleashing madness
which   is sometimes
uninvolved in contemporary mores
archetypal realities or graciousness

in the absence of extreme elegance
madness can set right in like
a burnin gauloise on japanese silk
though highly cultured
even the silk must ask
how to burn up discreetly

From *nappy edges*

purificar con miel

por tós los ritos que debo escribir
de derecha a izquierda/ de arriba abajo
o al revés/
el habla/ debe recorrerme enredá y disléxica por
el cerebro/ hastaque oigo tu voz
clara/ otra vez/

¿en qué otra vida/ fuiste un mandala?
¿acaso eres un "OM"?
¿es el shakti-pat/ tu estado metabólico regular/
en circunstancias ordinarias?
ay/ ahí voy de nuevo
admirándome/ sin querer/
invitando algo terrible/ un profuso *mot palabra son syllable*/
a sacudirse
entornoa mis golpes & azotes
tan húmedo/ sonríes/ recuerdo/ es arrogancia
& se acabó

esta/ purificación con miel
no es ná/ como la Pasión del Cristo/
que nos trajo la Cuaresma & dejamos la carne/
renunciamos a nuestra lujuria/ por sangre & bombones/
las pruebas de Mahoma trajeron el Ramadán/ & solo podemos
calmar nuestra sed de vida entre amanecer y atardecer/
& Buda/ bajo el bodhi/ repartió alegría por nuestros
tobillos
con tal de que nos liberáramos del resentimiento &
la impaciencia/ ahora bien Krishna/ tiene otro tipo de historia/
pero cabreros & cabreras/ pastores &
pastoras/
tós vienen con la purificación.

chastening with honey

by all rites i shd be writin
right to left/ upside down
or backwards/
speech/ shd run garbled & dyslexic thru my
brain/ til i hear yr voice
clearly/ again/

in some other/ life were you a mandala?
are you "OM"?
is shakti-pat/ yr regular metabolic status/
under ordinary circumstances?
oh/ there I go again
admirin myself/ unwittingly/
invitin some terribly/ lush *mot palabra son syllable*/
to flail
abt my bangs & lashes
so moist/ you smile/ i remember/ this is arrogance
& it's over

this/ chastening with honey
is nothin/ like the Passion of the Christ/
which brought us Lent & we give up meat/
quit our lust/ for blood & bonbons/
Mohammed's trials brought Ramadan/ & we may only
quench our thirst for life from dawn to dusk/
& Buddha/ neath the bo tree/ spread joy abt our
ankles
so long as we rid ourselves of resentment &
impatience/ now Krishna/ is another kind of story/
but goatherds & goatherdesses/ shepherds &
shepherdesses/
all come with chastening.

puedes/ curar esta lana/ mojarla
trenzarla hasta que puedas envolver con ella/ dos o tres
hilos cósmicos/ paralelos/ con ella
solo que/ no interrumpas el ritual
el salto desde maya al nirvana/ sobrecogimiento
sin querer/ arrogancia
& *je ne sais que ton insouciance*/ no podemos
bregar con la pasión/ con la destreza con que
nos asociamos con empleados civiles/ en Ibadán o en
Bogotá/
tengo mucha suerte
esta es la esencia de la vida/
te presentas/ con el calor de la Diosa
la ferocidad de Yavé/ el regocijo de Shiva/ la
astucia del Coyote/ el aliento deli-suave-cioso de
Obatalá/ como
si hubiera diferencia entre tu voz/ esta
miel/ que cae de
mi cuerpo/ & los colibríes salvajes de la selva pluvial
que se aparecen
por el tren A/ imaginan que eres/ polen de alguna flor
tropical
que ronda sobre Manhattan/ como el incienso del hermano
musulmán/
quizás si te quemara/ me calmaría/
los pájaros locos de
endorfinas/ podrían regresar al Amazonas/   piénsalo/
el fuego/ es un gran ritual de paso/   el polen &
la miel &
los pájaros que pasan por mi mejilla/ ay ay/ entiendo/
esta es la caída del Jardín.

you may/ sheer this wool/ wet it
braid it til you can wrap it round/ two or three
parallel/ cosmic strings/
just don't/ disrupt the ritual
the leap from maya to nirvana/ overwhelms
unwitting/ arrogance
& *je ne sais que ton insouciance*/ we
can't handle passion/ with the deftness
we associate with civil servants/ in Ibadan or
Bogota/
i am so lucky
this is the essence of life/ you
present yrself/ with the warmth of the Goddess
the ferocity of Yahweh/ the glee of Shiva/ the
cunning of Coyote/ the de-groovi-licious breath of
Obatala/ like
there was some difference tween yr voice/ this
honey/ fallin off
my body/ & wild hummingbirds from the rain forest
appear
by the A train/ imaginin you some/ tropical flower
pollen
hoverin over Manhattan/ like the Muslim brother's
incense/
maybe if i burn you up/ i'd calm down/
the endorphin crazed
birds/ cd go back to the Amazon/   think abt it/
fire/ is a great rite of passage/   the pollen &
the honey & the
flyin birds by my cheek/ oh oh/ i understand/
this is the fall from the Garden.

From *the love space demands*

envolver el viento

Candlemass 1980

las olas dejan las dunas esculpidas
arrastran & mueven por momentos
la arena sobre los caminos que
azotan las olas / atrápalo
captúralo / el viento deja señales
podemos leer el futuro
dibujos de arena
huella de arena / señales de costumbres
antiguas / envuelven el viento en
colores hermosos / fluyen como el mar
yacen desnudas en la cara de la luna
sus mareas / mecidas hasta dormir
por el cuchicheo en croché del
viento / de ese que te hormiguea
las mejillas / & la humildad que nos
hace llorar / una vez que conozcamos
al viento / un amante fugaz / que nos acaricia
el alma / envuelve al viento / y sujétalo.

wrapping the wind

Candlemass 1980

the waves leave the dunes sculpted
momentarily heaving & shifting
sand across the paths the
waves thrash / catch it
seize it / the wind leaves signs
we can read the future
sand drawings
sand prints / signals of ancient
ways / wrap the wind in
beautiful colors / flow like the sea
lie naked in the face of the moon
her tides / rocked to sleep
by the crocheted wisps of
wind / the kind that makes your
cheeks tingle / & humility that makes
us cry / once we've known the
wind / a fleeting lover / caressing our
souls / wrap the wind / & hold it tight.

From *ridin' the moon in texas*

en lo azul

en medio de la noche
hay un algo azul
algo azul en la noche
que me cubre
toca música
como hojas que no se han dejado/
mostrar   &
cuando no sé aonde estoy
cuando no sé cuándo te veré
qué hora es
me acuesto
en medio de la noche
cubierta de   este   azul
esta memoria de ti

los ojos de algunos ven marrón

los míos/ azul
a veces mueven/ incluso rocas
así que hasta parís no me resulta
tranquila/ me entretengo por el sena
un *homme noir*
azul como las caderas aterciopeladas
de un beguine de río pa mí
oscilo en la espesura
el aire en mis brazos
me guarda de la noche
podría entrar contigo
en lo azul
el peso eterno de tus brazos/
los míos llenos de cielo

_____

in the blueness

in the middle of the nite
is a blue thing
a blue thing in the nite
which covers me
makes music
like leaves that havent shown/
themselves   &
when i dont know where i am
when i dont know when i'll see you
what time it is
i lay
in the middle of the nite
covered up with   this   blueness
this memory of you

some men's eyes see hazel

mine see/ blue
sometimes it moves/ actually rocks
so even paris is not quiet
for me/ i linger by the seine
un homme noir
bein blue like the velvet hips
of river biguine for me
sway in the thickness
air on my arms
holdin me in from the nite i cd
enter with you
in the blueness
the forever weight of yr arms/
mine filled with sky

———

aquí estoy cargándote los labios
ahora tu melodía/ como me cantas
a veces hasta puedo ver correr las nubes
como el largo mar/ arrójame como las olas
arrójame como el viento/ que tu aliento sea
la tierra que gira/
sin parar nunca sin murmurar nunca
pero ay tan ruidosa

here i am carryin yr lips
yr tune now/ how you sing me
sometimes i even see clouds run
long like sea/ throw me like waves
throw me like wind/ make our breath
like the earth turnin/
never stoppin never hummin
but oh so loud

From *a daughter's geography*

7 tequilas después

unas cuantas calás de opio me calman
mi hija está en panamá
soy más peligrosa que noriega
según mi madre
que intentó llevar bourbon
dentro dela sala de tribunal aonde
me llamaron tó tipo de cosa menos
una madre incapaz/ me voy al ensayo
salgo hacia más entrevistas
ahora soy famosa   en realidá no
tengo vida/ tengo el tequila y los susurros
de mi hija que me dice
mami levántate
despiértate

7 tequilas gone

a few puffs of opium coolin me down
my daughter is in panama
i am more dangerous than noriega
accordin to my mother
who tried to carry bourbon
into the courthouse where they
called me everything but
an unfit mother / off to rehearsal
i go off for more interviews
now i am famous   i don't really
have a life/ i have tequila and whispers
of my child sayin
mami wake up
despierta-te

el escenario se queda oscuro

a las 4:30 AM
se levantó
movía los brazos & las piernas que la atrapaban
suspiró confirmando al hombre escultural
& se preparó un baño
de almizcle oscuro cristales egipcios
& agua florida pa quitarse su olor
pa lavarse el brillo
pa ver cómo las mariposas se hacen
lavaza & las piedras de fantasía
caen por entre
sus glúteos como guijarros suaves
en un arroyo de misuri
quietos en el agua
se convirtió en sí misma
ordinaria
mujer morena con trenzas
de piernas grandes & labios completos
normalita
con la intención seria de acabar sus
labores nocturnas
caminó rápido hasta su huésped
postrado entre sus sábanas & almohadas
     'tienes que irte ahora/ tengo
     mucho que hacer/ & no es posible
     con un hombre aquí/ toma tus pantalones/
     hay café en la estufa/ ha sido
     chévere/ pero no quiero volver a verte/
     ya tienes lo que querías/ ¿o no?'
& ella sonrío
él o murmuraba obscenidades sobre tipas locas
o se sentaba atontado
mientras ella repetía

the stage goes to darkness

at 4:30 AM
she rose
movin the arms & legs that trapped her
she sighed affirmin the sculptured man
& made herself a bath
of dark musk oil egyptian crystals
& florida water to remove his smell
to wash away the glitter
to watch the butterflies melt into
suds & the rhinestones fall beneath
her buttocks like smooth pebbles
in a missouri creek
layin in water
she became herself
ordinary
brown braided woman
with big legs & full lips
reglar
seriously intendin to finish her
night's work
she quickly walked to her guest
straddled on her pillows & began
 'you'll have to go now/ i've
 got a lot of work to do/ & i cant
 with a man around/ here are yr pants/
 there's coffee on the stove/ its been
 very nice/ but i cant see you again/
 you got what you came for/ didnt you'
& she smiled
he wd either mumble curses bout crazy bitches
or sit dumbfounded
while she repeated

'no podría levantarme/ con
un extraño en la cama/ por qué
no te vas pa tu casa'
le podrían haber pegado en la cabeza
o increpado verbalmente
pero eso nunca pasó
& los que cayeron presa de
el meneo de caderas pintadas con
muñecas que huelen a azahar y magnolia
no querían otra cosa
sino yacer entre sus muslos relucientes
& su plan era irse antes del amanecer
& ella había sido tan divina
devastadoramente rara la forma
enque su boca se acoplaba
& ahora estaba ahí de pie
una chica de color normal
llena dela misma indiferencia
maliciosa & viva que una negra
exhausta de apoyar a un trompetista en potencia
o de esperar junto a la ventana
    & ellos lo sabían
    & ellos huían
ella recogía sus guirnaldas &
joyas de la bañera
& se reía contenta o vengativa
guardaba sus rosas de seda junto a la cama
& cuando terminaba de escribir
el recuento de su hazaña en el diario
bordado de lirios y piedras de luna
se puso la rosa detrás de la oreja
& lloró hasta quedarse dormida.

'i cdn't possibly wake up/ with
a strange man in my bed/ why
dont you go home'
she cda been slapped upside the head
or verbally challenged
but she never waz
& the ones who fell prey to the
dazzle of hips painted with
orange blossoms & magnolia scented wrists
had wanted no more
than to lay between her sparklin thighs
& had planned on leavin before dawn
& she had been so divine
devastatingly bizarre the way
her mouth fit round
& now she stood a
reglar colored girl
fulla the same malice
livid indifference as a sistah
worn from supportin a wd be hornplayer
or waitin by the window
   & they knew
   & left in a hurry
she wd gather her tinsel &
jewels from the tub
& laugh gayly or vengeful
she stored her silk roses by her bed
& when she finished writin
the account of her exploit in a diary
embroidered with lilies & moonstones
she placed the rose behind her ear
& cried herself to sleep.

From *for colored girls who have considered suicide/ when the rainbow is enuf*

teléfonos y otros dioses
(para pedro pietri)

me siento muy insegura
ante la presencia de
carnívoros   aquellos
que me cobran intereses
por permitirles la entrada
a mis sueños en los que
insultan a visitantes sagrados
de este reino & a otras
criaturas que he encontrado
durante mi estadía entre ustedes

los vivos suelen no tener la moneda pa hacer
llamadas locales & el 911 es un producto
de la imaginación de los pillos mientras apalean
ojos de maricones & violan mujeres que nunca
han recibido amor ni han sido invitadas a comer

vuá pedir
que me corten el teléfono
cada noche esa trompeta
matancera me lleva al jardín
subterráneo   así puedo visitar los ritmos de la risa
    antes deque ella recuerde
       el tren A
& persiga con crueldá
a los pasajeros del metro
que leen anuncios de
eastern airlines
sin pedir el perdón
de una mujer que no puede encontrar
quimbombó fresco un martes por la noche
que se esforzó por ser una de las

telephones & other false gods
(for pedro pietri)

i feel very unsafe
in the presence of
meat-eaters   those
who charge me interest
for allowin them entrance
to my dreams where
they insult holy visitors
from this realm & other
creatures i have encountered
during my stay among you

the livin very often have no dime to make
local telephone calls & 911 is a figment of
muggers' imaginations while they bludgeon
faggots' eyes & rape women who have never
been loved or taken out to dinner

i'm gonna have
my phone turned off
every night that matancera's
trumpets take me to the underground
garden   so i can visit laughter's rhythms
   before she remembers
          the A train
& comes cruelly after
subterranean passengers
who read eastern airlines
advertisements
without askin forgiveness
from a woman who can't find
fresh okra on tuesday evenin
who tried very hard to be

buenas operadoras telefónicas de la bell
pero la despidieron porque era imposible
localizar seres humanos en el
directorio de la ciudad de nueva york

mientras tenga el teléfono descolgado
vuá ver esa avenida nostrand
que tiene una vela encendida & una luz de neón
se celebrará un mitin por el derecho
a que recojan la basura dos veces al año
& los niños que ya no hieden
al excedente de leche seca podrán jugar
en los patios sin que los acose
el policía de staten island
que se lo mete a su esposa por detrás
cuando tiene la oportunidad de patear
las bolas de un jodío negro saliva &
sueña con tostadas de frambuesa

los carnívoros perturban la melodía
causan gran angustia entre las mujeres
preñadas y los capullos ya no pueden
tolerar a jueces arbitrarios de concursos
de belleza que pronuncian mal los cuerpos africanos
por un viaje a las vegas
& muchas muchas noches marcadas de ginebra
con líderes sindicales ideales
que comen uvas & lechuga mientras
sus esposas hacen experimentos sadomasocas
con sirvientas de trinidad
que solo tienen 3 horas libres
pa limpiarse las heridas la
noche de los martes cuando no hay

good bell telephone operators
but got fired cuz it was impossible
to locate human beings in the
new york city directory

while my phone is off the hook
i'm goin to see that nostrand avenue
has a candle burnin & a neon light
rally will be held for the right
to semi-annual garbage collections
& children who no longer reek
of surplus dried milk can play
in backyards without bein molested
by the policeman from staten island
who makes it in his wife's ass
when he gets a chance to kick
a niggah's balls he salivates &
dreams of raspberry toast'ems

meat-eaters disrupt the melody
causin great anguish among pregnant
ladies and cocoons can no longer
tolerate arbitrary judges at beauty
contests mispronouncin african bodies
for a trip to las vegas
& many many gin-scarred nights
with ideal union leaders
eatin grapes & lettuce while
their wives do 's&m' experiments
on house girls from trinidad
who only get 3 hours off
to clean their wounds on
tuesday night when there

quimbombós frescos ni les permiten
bailar con hombres heterosexuales

cómo es que aún marcas mi número cuando
es obvio que solo contesto a los que no necesitan
teléfono pa llamar
     a los que deambulan
                   casualmente
por intensos anhelos
sin preguntar
por qué
los geechees portan navajas &
hablan solo/
con almas tropicales

no vuá
persistir en permitirte que me explotes
que conviertas mis sueños en pesadillas
de diablos de san francisco
con caras de juglares & de opio
no se le dará a mi blues de abstinencia
entradas a mi circo donde
tó es gratis
pero muy caro
pa aquellos que usan
nombres pa pagar
por la molestia de apoyar
un ego parásito/
a trompetistas & poetas
se les exhorta pa que
     dejen de
     postrarse
     frente a

is no fresh okra or dancin
allowed with heterosexual men

how can you keep dialin my number when
it's obvious i only answer those who need
no phone to call
           who can meander
                          casually
thru intense yearnings
without askin
why
geechees carry razors &
mingle w/
only tropical souls

i will not
persist in allowin you to exploit me
makin my dreams into nightmares
of san francisco devils
w/ minstrel faces & opium
withdrawal blues will not be given
tickets to my circus where
everythin is free
but very expensive
for those who use
their names to pay
for the trouble of
supportin parasitic
ego/
horn players & poets
will be discouraged from
       lyin
       prostrate
       before

figuras de cera &
las mujeres
aprenderán de nuevo
a ser como
el viento

no hay intermedios
cuando el disco se acaba celia cruz
& yo cantaremos a los familiarizados
con flores de 50 ¢
el parque central durante la semana
estará disponible pa amar árboles viejos
& recordarse
de hablar bien
de fats waller
quien pudo habernos
salvado

recordarse
recordarse   de hablar
bien
de
fats
waller
quien pudo habernos
salvado
de tonos de ocupado
autoimpuestos & de la peste
de los vampiros sueltos por las calles
que sufren de gota & la reacción
grabada a niños pequeños en
vagones caídos
las viejas
envueltas en bolsas de papel

        wax images &
women
            will once again learn
                to be like
                    the wind

    there are no intermissions
when the record is over celia cruz
& i will sing for those acquainted
with 50¢ flowers
        central park on weekdays
    will be available for lovin old trees
& rememberin
to speak highly
        of fats waller
        who cd have
            saved us

rememberin
rememberin   to speak
                highly
                    of
                fats
                    waller
        who cd have
        saved
        us
        from self-imposed
        busy signals & the stench
        of vampires loose on the streets
        sufferin with gout & tape-recorded
        reaction to small children in
        fallen wagons
old women
wrapped in paper bags

aún sueñan con
dientes de porcelana & con un lugar
pa lavarse
porque en sus sueños
pueden sostener a sus bebés & visitar a sus hijas
sin buscar una moneda pa llamar
encuentran que tós los circuitos
se fueron de vacaciones & la computadora
no tiene una lista de africanos
desplazaos que usan sus sobrenombres
pa escapar de los gritos de espíritus
que llaman que logran
visitar durante noches
de tifones huracanes apagones
&
otras
ocasiones
festivas
que
unen
familias
los desastres naturales prohíben a los amantes intercambiar #'s de
    teléfono
nos hacen esperar por alguien
olvidar
contestar   los timbres de la puerta
los teléfonos que suenan   nos suspenden
en el melodrama de las series de la tele
& las mujeres que no cocinan vegetales
frescos o les recuerdan a sus
hombres sobre el azahar & timbas seductoras
vienen a deshacer lo que está hecho
vienen a deshacer lo que está hecho
vienen a deshacer lo que está hecho

continue to dream of
porcelin teeth & a place
to wash
cuz in their dreams
they can hold babies & visit their daughters
w/ out looking for a dime to call
findin all the circuits
took a vacation & the computer
has no listin for displaced
africans usin aliases
to escape the cries of spirits
callin managin to
visit durin nights
of typhoons hurricanes blackouts
&
other
festive
occasions
that
bring
families
together
natural disasters prohibit lovers from exchangin phone #s
make us stay by someone
to forget
to answer   doorbells
ringin telephones   suspend us
in the melodrama of tv serials
& women who dont cook fresh
vegetables or remind their
men of orange blossoms & sultry conga drums
comin to un-do what's been done
comin to un-do what's been done
comin to un-do what's been done

huracanes   inundaciones   terremotos   & apagones
los desastres naturales nos hacen quedarnos con alguien
quédense con alguien
ocasiones festivas
quédense aquí

hurricanes   floods   earthquakes   & blackouts
natural disasters make us stay by someone
stay by someone
festive occasions
stay here

From *nappy edges*

los viejos

los viejos se reúnen
a eso de las 2:00 quizás las diez
a compartir empujones y soledad

el #1 siempre abre la puerta en albornoz
& malla de pelo/ invita al #2
se sientan en el portal/ las latas de cerveza
marrones y estáticas se ven raras en sus dedos
nudillos gruesos como pequeños cabos de hacha

el #3 está parado junto ala cerca
no hay césped aquí/
botellitas de vino/ el #4 dobla la esquina
el bolsillo superior izquierdo deshilachado/ los viejos
caminan con
fotos viejas   secretos   deseos

los viejos
se sientan encorvados pa cualquier lao
las manos penden entre las piernas
el #1 inclina el ala de su sombrero de paja/ el #3
estira la pierna coja
el #4 mastica la cerveza como si fuera un trozo de alimento
como si la tristeza fuera la regularidad de las chicas que pasan
el #2 asiente con la cabeza como el sauce blanco
el #4 se jala el bigote a las esquinas
de la boca/ son de por aquí/
se reúnen tós los días con fotos viejas   secretos   deseos

the old men

the old men meet
round 2:00 maybe ten to
share nudges & loneliness

#1 opens his door always in dressin gown
& stockin cap/ he invites #2 in
they sit on the porch/ brown stiff
beer cans sit awkward in their fingers
thick knuckles like small ax-handles

#3 leans on the picket fence
there is no grass here/
small wine bottles/ #4 walks round the corner
his top left pocket frayin/ the old men
walk with
old pictures   secrets   wishes

the old men
sit on either side of the stoop
hands dangle between their legs
#1 tips the brim of his straw hat/ #3
stretches a lame leg
#4 chews his beer cud-like
sadness like the regularity of young women passin
#2 nods his head same as the bleached willow
#4 pulls his moustache into the corners
of his mouth/ they're from round here/
they meet everyday with old pictures   secrets   wishes

From *nappy edges*

mujer torcida

la mujer no se para
derecha
nunca se ha parao
derecha/ siempre doblá
pa algún lao
torcía   girá
algo incliná hacia
una sombra de sí misma
parece que quiere
meterse toíta en la
tierra/ con la muerte
suya
tiene siempre algo sobre
los hombros/ que la empuja
fuera de sí misma
le corta las extremidades
es una maravilla el que pueda
estar de pie/ mirando
cómo está toa encorvá sobre sí misma

un saludo le puso la barbilla
bajo el brazo/ una
sonrisa le persiguió el cuello
por entre las piernas/
no es solo que no pueda pararse derecha/
no puede
apenas mantener el cuerpo
de otro fuera del suyo
& como tós sí podían
ver/ de inmediato/ esta
niña siempre se dobla

crooked woman

the woman dont stand up
straight
aint never stood up
straight/ always bent
some which a way
crooked   turned abt
slanted sorta toward
a shadow of herself
seems like she
tryin to get all in the
ground/ wit the death
of her
somethin always on her
shoulders/ pushin
her outta herself
cuttin at her limbs
a wonder she cd
stand at all/ seein
how she waz all curled over herself

a greetin sent her chin
neath her arm/ a
smile chased her neck
tween her legs/
waznt just she cdnt stand up straight/
she cdnt
hardly keep somebody
else's body outta hers
& since everyone cd
see/ immediately/ this
child always bends over
always twists

siempre se tuerce a
sí misma pa/
impedir pararse
la gente solo viene a jugar
con ella/ se divierten de lo lindo
mirando a la mujer torcía
hacer lo suyo/ & sus huesos
se quiebran
se resquebrajan/ se mutilan
a sí mismos hasta que ella
se ve tan rara
pa sí misma se/
encerró en un
armario/ donde conoció
a un hombre/ debió haberlo inventado/
porque él no sabía cómo se sentía
un hombre parao & derecho/ &

en la oscuridad
se retorcieron/ uno al otro hasta que
nadie pudo distinguirlos/ qué era eso
a lo que había que salirse del medio/ & ellos
nunca jamás hablaron/
de su condición.

round herself to/
keep from standin up
folks wd just go play
wit her/ get they kicks
watchin the crooked lady
do her thing/ & her bones
gotta crackin
shatterin/ mutilatin
themselves til she
waz lookin so weird
to herself she/
locked herself up in
a closet/ where she
met a man/ she musta made up/
cuz he didnt know what a stood
up straight man felt like/ &

in the dark
they curled round/ each other til
nobody cd tell anymore/ what to
get outta the way of/ & they
never once spoke/
of their condition.

From *from okra to greens*

vendar las heridas con ropa caliente

somos tan frágiles como las ligeras ramas de un árbol
colmadas de hielo en un día de invierno feroz
nos acomodamos junto a la escalera eléctrica de Penn Station
nos comemos nuestras curas & el camino / nuestro atún en latas
nuestra ropa en un carrito de compras de
alguna parte / la tienda de la gran manzana / no de
Balducci's ni de Jefferson Market
nos ponemos tres & cuatro vestidos a la vez
caminamos descalzos por la avenida 8
a veces cargamos con un olor peculiar
pero no es tan malo como el baño de mujeres
de Penn Station / la gente lleva
maletas & bolsos de viaje / aborda trenes
va a lugares / van robustos & pensativos
este lugar / nuestros harapos nos protegen
ves diseñé tó esto por mí misma / nadie
en ningún lugar se ve tan así esta
es mi belleza.

dressing our wounds in warm clothes

we're as fragile as slight tree limbs
laden with ice on a fierce winter day
we lay up by the escalator in Penn Station
eating our curds & whey / our tuna in cans
our clothes in a shopping cart from
somewhere / the big apple store / not
Balducci's or the Jefferson Market
we wear three & four dresses at a time
walk barefoot down 8th avenue
we have sometimes a peculiar odor
but no worse from the women's room
at Penn Station / people carry
suitcases & travel bags / take trains
go places / they're sturdy & mindful
this spot / our rags protect us
see i designed this myself / no one
anywhere looks quite like this
is my beauty.

From *ridin' the moon in texas*

annie la del crack

no puedo decir cómo se me ocurrió/ carajo
de alguna forma/ solo se me ocurrió/ &
escuché al señor decir cuán bella/ &
pura era esta niña mía/ & cuando
la miré sabía quel señor tenía
razón/ & era inocente/ tú sa'e/
libre de pecado/ & así es cómo se
la regalé a Cadillac Lee/ bueno/ cómo
explicarlo de otra manera

a quién amas quiero saber quiero saber
a quién amas quiero saber quiero saber

qué más puedo decir

a quién amas quiero saber quiero saber
a quién amas quiero saber quiero saber

no es como si ya tuviera pelo por
la chocha o algo así/ es muy chiquita
pa esas cosas/ & fijo que sabe/ que
a ella todavía no le baja ni ná/ pero un buen
amigo mío que vive cerca de la calle
28/ me dijo así a la picá
que no hay ná en el mundo como el olor
de una chocha virgen/ & que no hay ná en el
universo/ que sepa como una chocha nueva/ pero
eso lo dice mi pana/ & tu sa'e lo
difícil que es mantener un buen macho pa una
estos días/ aunque sé que tengo algo
dulce & caliente pa ofrecer/ aun
así/ quería darle a mi macho Cadillac
Lee/ algo que simplemente ya no tengo/

crack annie

i caint say how it come to me/ shit
somehow/ it just come over me/ & i
heard the lord sayin how beautiful/ &
pure waz this child of mine/ & when i
looked at her i knew the lord waz
right/ & she waz innocent/ ya know/
free of sin/ & that's how come i
gave her up to cadillac lee/ well/ how
else can i explain it

who do ya love i wanna know i wanna know
who do ya love i wanna know i wanna know

what mo could i say

who do ya love i wanna know i wanna know
who do ya love i wanna know i wanna know

it's not like she had hair round her
pussy or nothin/ she ain't old enough
anyway for that/ & we sho know/ she
aint on the rag or nothin/ but a real
good friend of mine from round 28th
street/ he tol me point-blank
wazn't nothin in the whole world smell
like virgin pussy/ & wazn't nothin in the
universe/ taste like new pussy/ now this
is my friend talkin/ & ya know how
hard it is to keep a good man fo yo self
these days/ even though i know i got
somethin sweet & hot to offer/ even
then/ i wanted to give my man cadillac
lee/ somethin i jus don't have no mo/

chocha nueva/ digo no estoy seca ni ná por
el estilo/ & todavía sé los músculos que
podría mover en mi chocha/ así &
asao pero lo que realmente quería/ que mi
macho/ Cadillac tuviera pa él/ era un poco
de chocha nueva/ & Berneatha era tan
linda & huelía tan bien/ aún después
de correr por ahí con los nenes/
mi Berneatha *mi vida*/ era dulce & estaba buena
recuerda esa canción "bien buena"
     tan buena mi beibi tan y tan buena
     que me eriza la espalda de arriba abajo
aaaay-oooh-ooooh-síííííííííí-síííííííííí-tan buena

bueno/ esa es mi hija/ la buena/ & puéh
Cadillac siempre ha bregao conmigo/ tú
sa'e con mi crack/ ay mami/ déjame decirte
lo cerca que estoy de Jesús gracias
a mi Cadillac/ déjame decirte/ que sin
ese macho yo ya estuviera entre
gusanos & mi tumba/ pero viste tenía
una chocha nueva/ era mi hija/ pérate
déjame refrasear / yo no tengo ninguna
chocha nueva/ asíque me busqué una / &
resulta que era Berneatha/ mi
hija/ & él me juró que me daría veinticinco
dólares & cincuenta pesos de crack enteritos/
lo que/ quisiera/ pero viste/ estoy con la pipa/
& no tengo ninguna chocha nueva/ & qué diferencia
podía
hacerle/ digo carajo/ no la pue'e preñar/
carajo/ solo tiene siete años
& estas marcas/ aquí/ por mis dedos

new pussy/ i mean it aint dried up or
nothin/ & i still know what muscles i
cd get to work in my pussy/ this-a-way
& that but what i really wanted/ my
man/ cadillac to have for his self/ waz some
new pussy/ & berneatha waz so
pretty & sweet smellin/ even after
she be out there runnin wit the boys/
my berneatha *vida/* waz sweet & fine
remember that song "so fine"

     so fine my baby's so doggone fine
    sends them thrills up & down my spine
whoah-oh-oh-yeah-yeaeaeah-so-fine

well/ that's my child/ *fine/* & well
cadillac always come thru for me/ ya
know wit my crack/ oh honey/ lemme tell
ya how close to jesus i get thanks
to my cadillac/ lemme say now/ witout
that man i'd been gone on to
worms & my grave/ but see i had me
some new pussy/ waz my daughter/ lemme
take that back/ i didn't have none/
any new pussy/ so i took me some/ & it
just happened to be berneatha/ my
daughter/ & he swore he'd give me twenty-five
dollars & a whole fifty cent of crack/
whenever/ i wanted/ but you know/ i'm on the pipe/
& i don't have no new pussy/ & what difference/
could it
make/ i mean shit/ she caint get pregnant/
shit/ she only seven years old
& these scratches/ heah/ by my fingers

ahí/ fue de donde se agarró mi hija
de mí/ cuando el cabrón/ de Cadillac/ la agarró
como si no tuviera ninguna chocha nueva
ná/ ella solo me miraba &
me gritaba/ "mami/ mami ayúdame/ ayuda
me"/ & lo que hice fue agarrarla
más fuerte/ como si pudiera impedir
que su sangre circule/como si pudiera
evitarle el dolor/ pero no/ así no fue
como pasó la cosa/ pa ná fue así/
créeme/ tengo las cicatrices donde las
uñas de mi hija me rompieron la piel
& luego/ cuando él terminó con mi
nena/ Cadillac/ brincó & me dijo
que cubriera la chocha de mi hija/ con
cocaína/ pa que ella no sintiera
más/ digo/ porqué no lo hiciste
antes/porqué esperar hasta que acabaras/
pa protegerla/ él dice/ antes de que te
tumbe & te dé algo de lo mismo/
no sa'es/ tienes que oírlas
gritar antes de darle un poquito de
dulce/ & mi chiquita lo escuchó
tó/ mi hija sangró tó esto/ & tó
lo que pude hacer era buscar más crack
de los cincuenta que me dio Cadillac
pero/ no lo buscaba pa mí
lo sabe Jesús/ los quería pa
Berneatha/ pa que no tuviera que
recordar/ no tuviera que
recordar/ ná de ná/ pero vi marcas oscuras
& púrpura
en su hombro/ donde la había sujetado pa
Cadillac/ soy su mai & la sujeté

that's/ where my child held onto
me/ when the bastard/ cadillac/ took
her like she wazn't even new pussy at
all/ she kept lookin at me &
screamin/ "mommy/ mommy help me/ help
me"/ & all i did waz hold her
tighter/ like if i could stop her
blood from circulation/ if i could stop
her from hurtin/ but no/ that aint how
it went down at all/ nothin like that/
trust me/ i got scars where my
daughter's fingernails broke my skin
& then/ when he waz finished wit my
child/ cadillac/ he jump up & tell me
to cover my child's pussy/ wit some
cocaine/ so she wdn't feel nothin no
mo/ i say/ why ya aint done
that befo/ why ya wait til ya done/
to protect her/ he say/ befo i lay
you down & give ya some of the same/
dontcha know/ ya haveta hear
em scream befo ya give em any
candy/ & my lil girl heard all
this/ my child bled alla this/ & all i
could do waz to look for some more crack
wit the fifty cadillac done give
me/ but/ i wazn't lookin for it for
me/ jesus knows/ i wanted it for
berneatha/ so she wouldn't haveta
remember/ she wouldn't have to
remember/ nothin at all/ but i saw dark purple
colored marks
by her shoulder/ where i held her down for
cadillac/ i'm her mother & i held her

& si me matan/ siempre sabré/
que merodearé por el infierno hablando
de chocha nueva/ & veré la sangre de
mi hija esparcida en sus muslos/ los hombros
de mi hija morados por el amor de
su madre/ Jesús sálvame/ llévame
Jesús/ ahora/ dios toma mi alma & haz
tu voluntad con ella/ dios ten
misericordia/ creía que Berneatha era
como yo/ que podía aguantarlo tó/ tú
sa'e/ que no hay ná que pueda con la voluntá de la gente
de color/ pero señor estaba
equivocada/ esas marcas de mi niña/ no/
no las marcas/ de Cadillac/ las cicatrices
de mis dedos/ manchones
morados & azules/ medianoche toda rubí en lenox
avenue a las 7:30 los domingos/ aquel silencio
pesado/ aquella crueldá/ no lo aguanto
más/ así que señor lánzame al infierno antes que
Berneatha haya crecido/ lo hará ella
misma/ solita/ riendo
& empujándome/ & acechándome &
fastidiándome/ diciendo/ eres madre/ qué
claje madre eres/ puta/ dime/
ahora/ mamita qué claje madre/ eres/ mamita
mamita/

digo/ vi a Etta James en sus ojos/ lo
sé/ vi el blues en sus ojos/ un
blues/ virulento/ al acecho
no acepta otra contestación que un sí a mi
blues/ una canción de una Etta James/ un
blues cascarrabias/ un blues que nace de
necesitar & añorar/ necesitar & añorarte a

& if ya kill me/ i'll always know/
i'm gonna roam around hell talkin
bout new pussy/ & see my child's
blood caked bout her thighs/ my child's
shoulders purple wit her mother's
love/ jesus save me/ come get me
jesus/ now/ lord take my soul & do
wit it what ya will/ lord have
mercy/ i thought berneatha waz like
me/ that she could take anythin/ ya
know/ caint nothin kill the will of the
colored folks/ but lord i waz
wrong/ them marks on my child/ no/
not the marks/ from cadillac/ the scars
from my fingers/ purple & blue
blotches/ midnight all ruby on lenox
avenue at 7:30 on sundays/ that heavy
quiet/ that cruelty/ i caint take
no mo/ so lord throw me into hell befo
berneatha is growed/ she do it
herself/ all by herself/ laughin
& shovin me/ & prowlin &
teasin/ sayin/ you a mother/ what
kinda mother are you/ bitch/ tell me/
now/ mommy what kinda mother/ are you/ mommy/
mommy/

i say/ i heard etta james in her eyes/ i
know/ i heard the blues in her eyes/ an
unknown/ virulent blues/ a stalkin
takin no answer but yes to me
blues/ a song of a etta james/ a
cantankerous blues/ a blues born of
wantin & longin/ wantin & longin for

ti/ mami/ o Etta Mae/
canción de un blues de segunda mano
que cuelga de su aliento/ solo
un blues frágil & nuevo
apenas cerca de ná/ cepto esos ojos
& digo/ oí a un montón de Etta James
en sus ojos/ por tós sus ojos/
así que ven acá Annie

así que cuéntaselo todo a mamá

cuéntaselo todo a mamá
todo todito
todo todito

díselo a mamá

you/ mama/ or etta mae/
song of a ol hand me down blues
hangin by its breath/ alone
a fragile new blues
hardly close to nowhere/ cept them eyes
& i say/ i heard a heap of etta james
in them eyes/ all over them eyes/
so come on Annie

so tell mama all about it

tell mama all about it
all about it
all about it

tell mama

From *the love space demands*

sobre atlanta

como es negro & pobre
desapareció
el nombre se perdió   no se jugaron los partidos
nadie lo acuesta a dormir por las noches/ ni borra restos
de pan de maíz & sirope de sus dedos
de las esquinas de su boca
porque es negro & pobre/ no solo
se fue
se desvaneció un día
& su sangre absorbe lo que ya es rojo
en atlanta

no hubo sogas esta vez   ni alquitrán & plumas
no hubo ningunos desfiles de sábanas fuegos & cruces
ná/ ni rastro

literas vacías
madres que olvidan & cocinan de más los domingos
se fue/ desapareció
porque es negro y pobre   se fue
tomó un bus/ jamás se supo de él

pero alguien escuchó a un niño gritar
            & siguió de largo
niños que desaparecen/ en algún lugar del bosque/ en decadencia
se van sin más/ desaparecidos/ en atlanta

las madres siempre están en la ventana mirando
no hay nadie que desaparezca frente a sus ojos
pero quién sabe lo que podríamos hacer
cuando somos negros & pobres

about atlanta

cuz he's black & poor
he's disappeared
the name waz lost   the games werent played
nobody tucks him in at night/ wipes traces
of cornbread & syrup from his fingers
the corners of his mouth
cuz he's black & poor/ he's not
just gone
disappeared one day
& his blood soaks up what's awready red
in atlanta

no ropes this time   no tar & feathers
werent no parades of sheets fires & crosses
nothing/ no signs

empty bunkbeds
mothers who forget & cook too much on sundays
just gone/ disappeared
cuz he's black & poor   he's gone
took a bus/ never heard from again

but somebody heard a child screaming
            & went right on ahead
children disappearing/ somewhere in the woods/ decaying
just gone/ disappeared/ in atlanta

mothers are always at the window watching
caint nobody disappear right in fronta yr eyes
but who knows what we cd do
when we're black & poor

no estamos aquí no/ ¿cómo podríamos desaparecer?
¿quién escucharía nuestros gritos?

di que fue un hombre con placa & algo de dulce
di que fue un hombre con placa & algo de dinero
di que fue un maniaco
podría ser más que palos y piedras
tiene que ser más que barras y estrellas
los niños no pueden jugar a la guerra cuando viven en una.
no pueden morirse de a mentiras/ porque mueren de a de veras
no pueden imaginarse lo que serán/ porque no lo harán
solo se irán/ desaparecidos

ay maría no me llores & no te me quejes
ay maría no me llores & no te me quejes
GRITA digo GRITA
porque somos negros & pobres & tenemos que desaparecer

no podemos encontrarlos   jesús no puede encontrarlos
hasta que rezuman en la tierra
padre rezuma en la tierra
sus huesos a punto de desaparecer
sus vidas nunca han sido
sangran donde la tierra ya es roja
mueren porque tomaron el autobús
& mamá no puede ver tan lejos desde la ventana
el portal no va de aquí a la eternidad
& se han ido
desaparecidos sin más

pero alguien los oyó gritar
alguien trituró esos huesos de niños

we aint here no way/ how cd we disappear?
who wd hear us screaming?

say it was a man with a badge & some candy
say it was a man with a badge & some money
say it was a maniac
cd be more n sticks n stones
gotta be more than stars n stripes
children caint play war when they in one.
caint make believe they dyin/ when they are
caint imagine what they'll be/ cuz they wont
just gone/ disappeared

oh mary dont you weep & dont you moan
oh mary dont you weep & dont you moan
HOLLAR i say HOLLAR
cuz we black & poor & we just disappear

we cant find em   jesus cant find em
til they seepin in soil
father reekin in soil
they bones bout disappeared
they lives aint never been
bleeding where the earth's awready red
dyin cuz they took a bus
& mama caint see that far out her window
the front porch dont go from here to eternity
& they gone
just disappeared

but somebody heard them screaming
somebody crushed them children's bones

alguien que camina debería arrastrarse
por matar a quienes nunca fueron
porque somos negros & pobres/ solo desaparecemos

sin importar cuán amables/ sin importar cuán tranquilos
solo desaparecidos
vengo ya mismo ma
voy pala tienda mamita linda
te veo después abu
te llamo cuando llegue, mami

& el suelo fluye rojo con nuestros muertos en atlanta
porque alguien no dudó en
triturar sus huesitos/ en estrangular sus frágiles lamentos
porque somos negros & pobres
        nuestra sangre absorbe el sucio
        mientras desaparecemos

las mamás siguen mirando afuera desde la puerta
dicen "dónde estará mi hijo/ me pregunto
                dónde estará mi hija"
no arregla la cama porque sabe
que somos negros & pobres
& solo desaparecemos/ nos vamos

ay maría no me llores & no te me quejes
ay maría no me llores & no te me quejes
me pregunto dónde estará mi hijo
me pregunto dónde estará mi hija

ná/ sin rastro
en atlanta

somebody's walkin who shd be crawling
for killing who aint never been
cuz we black & poor/ we just be gone

no matter how sweet/ no matter how quiet
just gone
be right back ma
going to the store mother dear
see ya later nana
call ya when I get there mama

& the soil runs red with our dead in atlanta
cuz somebody went right on ahead
crushing them lil bones/ strangling them frail wails
cuz we black & poor
      our blood soaks up dirt
      while we disappearing

mamas keep looking out the door
saying "i wonder where is my child/ i wonder
            where is my child"
she dont turn the bed back cuz she knows
we black & poor
& we just disappear/ be gone

oh mary dont you weep & dont you moan
oh mary dont you weep & don't you moan
i wonder where is my child
i wonder where is my child

nothing/ no signs
in atlanta

From *a daughter's geography*

a quién le hace falta un corazón

en algún lugar de soweto hay una niñita
es trigueña flaca & tiene miedo
come cartón a veces porque tiene hambre
& simula que es pan y carne
carne caliente con mantequilla & sal
entre dos lascas de pan
tiene cuatro años
come pasto a veces porque tiene hambre
las vacas comen pasto también las cabras
piensa que es un animal
no hay nadie cerca que la abrace
que la llame por su nombre, "Ndekedehe", cuenta
una historia como la de cenicienta o blancanieves
o quizás ya alguien le habrá contado
sobre cenicienta, así que a los cuatro años
ha decidido que es mejor ser una criatura de cuatro patas
que una que se para en dos
con picanas & rifles
pa aterrorizar a los niños & desgraciarnos
a tós / quién puede levantarse en sus propios pies /
pa ver el apartheid como si fuera otra película de toda la noche.

who needs a heart

somewhere in soweto there's a small girl
she's brown thin & frightened
she eats cardboard sometimes she's hungry
& she makes believe it's bread & meat
warm meat with butter & salt
tween two slices of bread
she's four years old
she eats grass sometimes she's hungry
cows eat grass so do goats
she thinks she's an animal
there's no one around to hold her
call her name, "Ndekedehe," tell
her a story like rose red & rose white
or maybe someone awready told
her about rose white & so at four
she's decided it's better to be a four-legged creature
than the kind that stand on two legs
with cattle prods & rifles
terrifying children & disgracing
all of us / who can stand on our own two feet /
watching apartheid as if it were another all-night movie.

From *ridin' the moon in texas*

pueblo de watts

de aonde venimos, a veces, la belleza
flota entre nosotros como las nubes
como las hojas crujen en la brisa
y el pan de maíz y la barbacoa giran por la puerta trasera
y nos tientan los sentidos mientras cae el sol.

sueños y memorias descansan por las cercas
los acentos de Texas se aceleran como motores
personalizados que brillan poderosos como los brazos
que nos sujetan fuerte negros y fragantes
nos recuerdan que alguna vez dormimos y amamos
al aroma de las magnolias y frangipanis
alguna vez cuando miramos al cielo
podíamos ver algo tan encantador como las sonrisas
de nuestros hijos blancas y relucientes sin miedo ni vergüenza
chicas con trenzas tan preciosas como el oro
se dieron cuenta que el sexo no solo está en que te toquen
sino también en el vaivén de sus caderas la luz que cae por
una mejilla trigueña o en el mero movimiento del dedo
al labio muchos labios que invitan besos sureños
y en la onda como cualquier hermano espigado al calor
de un domingo relajado rico como una mamá grande aún
enamorá de la idea del amor cómo jugamos al amor
aun arriesgando tó el sentido común porque somos tan fantasiosos
como cualquier quimera o flores mágicas en las quelos pechos
    tientan
y disimulan al retumbar atropellao en nuestros corazones
mientras la música que somos
blues acérrimos voces en tono grave que canturrean
directo desde Compton melodías tan bellas
navegan Harbor Freeway bien maleantes
tiran besos a extraños quenolo serán por mucho tiempo
nos cantábamos pa nosotras mismas Mamie Khalid Sharita

people of watts

where we come from, sometimes, beauty
floats around us like clouds
the way leaves rustle in the breeze
and cornbread and barbecue swing out the backdoor
and tease all our senses as the sun goes down.

dreams and memories rest by fences
Texas accents rev up like our engines
customized sparkling powerful as the arms
that hold us tightly black n fragrant
reminding us that once we slept and loved
to the scents of magnolia and frangipani
once when we looked toward the skies
we could see something as lovely as our children's
smiles white n glistenin' clear of fear or shame
young girls in braids as precious as gold
find out that sex is not just bein' touched
but in the swing of their hips the light fallin cross
a softbrown cheek or the movement of a mere finger
to a lip many lips inviting kisses southern
and hip as any one lanky brother in the heat
of a laid back sunday rich as a big mama still
in love with the idea of love how we play at lovin'
even riskin' all common sense cause we are as fantastical
as any chimera or magical flowers where breasts entice
and disguise the racing pounding of our hearts
as the music that we are
hard core blues low bass voices crooning
straight outta Compton melodies so pretty
they nasty cruising the Harbor Freeway
blowin' kisses to strangers who won't be for long
singing ourselves to ourselves Mamie Khalid Sharita

Bessie Jock Tookie MaiMai Cosmic Man Mr. Man
Keemah y el resto cortejando en serio
rapeando un inglés que nos inventábamos mientras cantábamos
convertíamos los nombres en verbos las trenzas en coronas
y siempre cazábamos sueños de un horizonte
esparció con huesos y carne de aquellos de nosotros
queno sobrevivimos cuyas sonrisas y ojos profundos
y oscuros nos ayudan a continuar a ver
que hay mucha vida aquí.

Bessie Jock Tookie MaiMai Cosmic Man Mr. Man
Keemah and all the rest seriously courtin'
rappin' a English we make up as we go along
turnin' nouns into verbs braids into crowns
and always fetchin' dreams from a horizon
strewn with bones and flesh of those of us
who didn't make it whose smiles and deep
dark eyes help us to continue to see
there's so much life here.

dama de rojo

me senté una noche // caminaba toda una pensión
gritaba/ lloraba/ el fantasma de otra mujer
que no tenía lo que yo no tenía
quería brincar fuera demis huesos
& acabar conmigo misma
déjenme quieta
& irme con el viento
era demasiado
caí entumecida
hasta que el único árbol que podía ver
me puso entre sus ramas
me abrazó en la brisa
me hizo rocío mañanero
ese frío al romper el día
el sol me envolvió & oscilaba luz rosada por tós lados
el cielo se postró sobre mí como un millón de hombres
tenía frío/ ardía de fiebre/ una niña
& tejer prendas sin parar pa la luna
con mis lágrimas

encontré a dios en mí misma
& la amé/ la amé con fiereza

lady in red

i sat up one nite // walkin a boardin house
screamin/ cryin/ the ghost of another woman
who waz missin what i waz missin
i wanted to jump up outta my bones
& be done wit myself
leave me alone
& go on in the wind
it waz too much
i fell into a numbness
til the only tree i cd see
took me up in her branches
held me in the breeze
made me dawn dew
that chill at daybreak
the sun wrapped me up swingin rose light everywhere
the sky laid over me like a million men
i waz cold/ i waz burnin up/ a child
& endlessly weavin garments for the moon
wit my tears

i found god in myself
& i loved her/ i loved her fiercely

From *for colored girls who have considered suicide/ when the rainbow
is enuf*

coro del nuevo mundo

nuestra lengua   es táctil
de color & húmeda
nuestras lenguas hablan
estas palabras
bailamos
estas palabras
las cantamos como si creyéramos en ellas/
        hacerles cosas arrastrar golpear & navegarlas
a ellas/ vivirlo/ el poema
nuestras visiones son nuestras
nuestra verdad no es menos violenta que lo necesario
pa hacer que
los sueños de nuestras hijas
sean tan reales como losdeloshombres
&
la tierra murmura una canción de su autoría…
porque
tenemos una hija/ mozambique
tenemos un hijo/ angola
nuestros gemelos
salvador & johannesburgo/ no pueden hablar
la misma lengua
pero peleamos contra los viejos de siempre/ en el nuevo mundo
tenemos tanta hambre pa la mañana
intentamos alimentar a nuestros hijos con el sol
pero hace mucho tiempo/ abordamos naves/ encadenaos en
profundidades marinas nuestros espíritus/ besamos la tierra
del lado atlántico de nicaragua costa rica
nuestros labios trazaron los bordes de cuba puerto rico
charleston & savannah/ en haití
nos abrazamos &
hicimos niños del nuevo mundo

new world coro

our language   is tactile
colored & wet
our tongues speak
these words
we dance
these words
sing em like we mean it/
      do it to em stuff drag punch & cruise it
to em/ live it/ the poem/
our visions are our own
our truth no less violent than necessary
to make
our daughters' dreams
as real as mensis
&
the earth hums some song of her own . . .
cuz
we have a daughter/ mozambique
we have a son/ angola
our twins
salvador & johannesburg/ cannot speak
the same language
but we fight the same old men/ in the new world
we are so hungry for the morning
we're trying to feed our children the sun
but a long time ago/ we boarded ships/ locked in
depths of seas our spirits/ kisst the earth
on the atlantic side of nicaragua costa rica
our lips traced the edges of cuba puerto rico
charleston & savannah/ in haiti
we embraced &
made children of the new world

pero los viejos nos escupieron/ encadenaron nuestras extremidades
los viejos nos escupieron/encadenaron nuestras extremidades
pero solo por un minuto…
verás al resto de nosotros en luanda o al resto de nosotros en
    chicago.

but old men spit on us/ shackled our limbs
old men spit on us/shackled our limbs
for but a minute . . .
you'll see us in luanda or the rest of us in chicago.

From *a daughter's geography*

camina, brinca, vuela

mami puedo contarte algo
mami te puedo compartir algo
mami puedo contarte algo
con permiso mami te puedo compartir algo
mami mami podrías verme
mami puedes verme ahora
mami puedo contarte algo
mami necesitamos darle a jesús
algo ha estado en una cueva tres días
qué le traemos a jesús / mami
puedo enseñarte algo / con permiso
mami / en la escuela nadie me quiere /
mami puedo contarte algo
mami puedo contarte algo / tenemos
que comprarle un regalo de cumple al Pato Donald /
cumplió cincuenta años / mami qué crees
que le gustaría a Donald / mami
puedo contarte algo / mami

mami mami mami

puedo contarte algo / tengo
27 postales de san valentín / tós en la escuela
me aman / a mí / mami puedo contarte algo
con permiso mami puedo enseñarte algo
mami esto es pa ti ábrelo
ahora / te gusta mami / mami
puedo enseñarte algo / mami
puedo contarte algo / estos
son floreros distintos violetas
& cardos / mami sabías eso /

walk, jump, fly

mommy can i tell you something
mommy can i share you something
mommy can i tell you something
excuse me mommy can i share you something
mommy mommy would you watch me
mommy can you see me now
mommy can i tell you something
mommy we need to give jesus
something he's been in a cave three days
what should we get jesus / mommy
can i show you something / excuse me
mommy / nobody likes me at school /
mommy can i tell you something
mommy can i tell you something / we
have to get Donald Duck a birthday present /
he's fifty years old / mommy what do
you think Donald would like / mommy
can i tell you something / mommy

mommy mommy mommy

can i tell you something / i got
27 valentines / everybody at school loves
me / me / mommy can i tell you something
excuse me mommy can i show you something
mommy this is for you mommy open it
now / mommy do you like it / mommy
can i show you something / mommy
can i tell you something / these
are different flowers vases violets
& thistles / mommy did you know that /

mami mami mami

mami puedo preguntarte algo / por favor
mami puedo preguntarte algo / mami
me amas / ay qué bueno me alegro mami
te amo mami / mami puedo preguntarte algo
mami solo quiero preguntarte una cosa
más / mami ¿puedes volar?

——————

mommy mommy mommy

mommy can i ask you something / please
mommy can i ask you something / mommy
do you love me / oh good i'm glad mommy
i love you mommy / mommy can i ask you something
mommy i just wanna ask you one more
thing / mommy can you fly?

From *ridin' the moon in texas*

la fama a cuatro patas

1)

escribí en san francisco en
un tablón 4 por 12
contrachapado sin acabar
cubierto de cuadros rosados & amarillos
conocía a 3 personas
    un amigo en baltimore
    una amiga encinta
    un amigo enamorao
escribí alimentando a mis yoes
sin lengua
    sin boca
que pudiéramos entender/
              "¿qué pasa aquí?"
jóvenes en volkys vintage tocan la bocina
los blanquitos de texas piden perdón
los poetas alucinan con los pies en el agua helada & pura
ennotados como los bailarines brincan más allá de la gravedad en
   el lomo
un estudiante cuelga un columpio de 16 pies junto a mi puerta
me agarro a la cintura de un veterano en una harley-davidson
en la lluvia/ quiere beber poesía
se conforma con una coors

2)

la fama se monta en la máquina de escribir en nueva york
      "la cinta magenta no es suficiente
      tampoco la naranja o la turquesa
      no tienes cintas negras
         no tienes ná ordinario
      nunca he imaginado 3 amantes en un día
      le dije a un crítico que sufre de neoplasia
      puta/ a quién te crees que le hablas

fame on all fours

1)

i wrote in san francisco on
a 4 by 12 board
plywood unfinished
covered with pink & yellow squares
i knew 3 people
    one friend in baltimore
    a friend with child
    one friend in love
i wrote feedin my selves
with no tongue
    no mouth
that we might understand/
                  "what's happenin here?"
yng men in vintage vw's honk horns
crackers from texas apologize
poets hallucinate all feet in water chilled & pure
high as dancers leap beyond gravity in the tenderloin
a student hangs a 16 ft. swing by my door
i hold the waist of a veteran on a harley-davidson
in the rain/ he wants to drink poetry
settles for coors

2)

fame gets on the typewriter in new york/
    "the magenta ribbon wont do
    nor orange nor aqua
    have you no black ribbon
      have you nothin ordinary
    i've never imagined 3 lovers in a day
    told a critic he suffers from malignancy
    bitch/ who are you talking to

trabajo tós los días/ mis hijos son analfabetos
ni tan siquiera adoran a clarabelle
tengo una maidenform pa tó/ los negros
ya no tienen sentido táctil del algodón
nos ha superado el nilón/ vivimos en una caja
con la canción del show de phil donahue & cuál es mi
    profesión
no tienes ná ordinario"
ella pone caras
    "no tienes cintas negras"

3)
quizás tallulah me ayude/ aunque soy una jodía negra
quizás faulkner saldrá de la tierra
digo porque soy una jodía negra y deben dejarme quieta
quizás appollinaire logre que tuerza la
bastilla en mi lengua
baudelaire fijo me seducirá
me parezco a ella

pero

la fama
se sienta en la máquina de escribir   ríe
se burla/ da empujones/ de hecho saca sangre
mis yoes no tienen lenguas ni voces
algunos/ no tienen piernas/ ni brazos
siempre estamos sujetos a la emboscada
la fama me envía realidades nulas
a islas diseñadas pa lo criminal
lo peculiar/ lo socialmente defectuoso/ el poeta
¿qué debo hacer allí?
hacer que dumas me lleve a por ahí en una silla de ruedas
me enviará anna akhmatova algún amante de sobra o dos
edith piaf tiene más que ver con billie holiday que lo que

            i work every day/ my kids are illiterate
            they dont even cherish clarabelle
            i've a maidenform everything/ niggahs
            have no tactile sense of cotton any more
            we've been overtaken by qiana/ live in a box
            with the gong show phil donahue & what's my line
            have you nothin ordinary"
she grimaces
            "have you no black ribbons"

    3)
maybe tallulah will help me/ tho i'ma niggah
maybe faulkner will get out the ground
say cuz i'm a niggah i shd be left alone
maybe apollinaire will have me twirl the
bastille on my tongue
baudelaire assuredly will seduce me
i look like her

but

fame
sits on the typewriter   laughing
she jeers/ shoves/ draws blood actually
my selves have no tongues no voices
some/ no legs/ arms
we are always subject to ambush
fame sends my invalid realities
to islands designed for the criminal
the peculiar/ the socially defective/ the poet
what shall i do there?
have dumas roll me round in a wheel chair
will anna akhmatova send me a leftover lover or two
edith piaf has more to do with billie holiday than

sabemos/ & viene de camino
las horas de visita son de ahora hasta entonces los sábados
los domingos estamos libres

4)
la puerta principal está rota/ vidrio por tós lados
la fama deshace los adoquines de mi calle/
mi piel tiene erupciones
veo al hombre del sonido cada vez que puedo
vuá a flatbush 4 veces por semana
el yo que no tiene boca
debe ser persuadida & mimada
no sabe que somos especiales & no tiene forma
de hacer arreglos/
es silente
estoy aquí pa traducir
los sonidos que hace/ el tartamudeo atroz
palabras completas/ actos de agresión
ella es mi palabra

cuando la fama se sienta en mi máquina de escribir
tengo que cegarle los ojos/ taparme las orejas
no puede leer/ no entiende estos reinos
en los que entro/ la fama se sienta suelta en el piso
con un abanico trinitario/ las caderas de una cuera en celo
las voces que alcanzo/ porque
tós mis yoes no han bailado todavía
mis yoes sin gestos/ sin apetito elegido
sin garganta pa gritar/ tengo que dejar que crezcan
la fama se sienta en mi máquina de escribir
podrá patear & gritar/ intimidarme con acusaciones
histéricas/ pero
     mis voces sin lenguaje
     mis bailarines sin espacio

we know/ & she's coming
visting hours are from now til then on saturday
sunday we are free

4)
my front door's broken/ glass is everywhere
fame's undoing the cobblestones on my street/
my skin with eruptions
i see the sound man when ever i can
i go to flatbush 4 times a week
my self who has no mouth
must be coaxed & pampered
she does not know we are special & has no way
to make arrangements/
she is silent
i am here to translate
noises she makes/ gross stutters
whole words/ acts of aggression
she is my word

when fame sits on my typewriter
i must bind her eyes/ block my ears
she cannot read/ does not understand these realms
i enter/ fame sits undone on the floor
with a trinidadian fan/ the hips of a warm trollop
the voices i am reaching/ for
all my selves who have not yet danced
my selves with no gesture/ no chosen appetite
no throat to scream/ i must grow them out
fame may sit on the typewriter
she can kick & holler/ intimidate me with hysterical
accusations/ but
	my voices with no language
	my dancers with no space

me alimentan & me sostienen
vestida en la melodía o no
& la fama se sienta junto al escritorio
una perra sospechosa de sus orígenes
ella eres tú que no tienes necesidad de mí
ella eres tú con bocas historia
poder & sin memoria de lo desconocido
soy la voz de los yoes que no han/ aprendido a hablar
mis sueños mudos & sordos se hacen realidá aquí
mis hijas silentes
la razón por la que hablo

they feed me & carry me
clothed in melody or not
& fame sits by the desk
a dog of suspicious origins
she is you who have no need of me
she is you with mouths history
power & no memory of the unknown
i am the voice of my selves who have not/ learned to speak
my mute & deaf dreams come thru here
my silent daughters
why i speak at all

From *nappy edges*

poema lagarto

una iguana de dogón
un ojo abierto que me ve
ve mis sueños
treparse
como los pies de
david rousseve
desde mis pechos finos
hechos en rahway
los negros en puentes
brillantes/ los admiran
tanto/ se detienen
se pelan los dientes riendo
brillan aguantan la lujuria
lo único que saben es que más vale
que no juegue/ con ellos

nadan encima de sí mismos
por el río grande en
época de lluvia/ así que
mis piernas tientan
al guardia fronterizo
          "¿danza de apareamiento de jalisco?"
"no, cosecha de sonora"/ pies
agua
ritmo/
¡llegué!
¡¡tierra!!
tatuada como
sus brazos lagartos que
se deslizan encima
del cruce mojado
hacia ácaba
hacia mí/ como

214

lizard poem

a dogon iguana
one eye open seeing me
seeing my dreams
creep like david
rousseve's feet
from my finely cut
pecs rahway built
niggah's on gleamin'
bridges/ admire so
much/ they stop
smile snaggle-toothed
gleamin' lust gleamin'
all they know I bettah
not toy with/ they dreams

swimmin' top themselves
by the rio grande in
rainy season/ so
my calves tease
the border patrol
      "jalisco courtin' dance?"
"no, sonora harvest"/ toes
water
ritmo/
made it!
land!!
tattooed like
his arms lizards
slitherin' on top
the wet crossin'
toward ácaba
toward me/ like

la seda / su piel exige
tacto humano
¿la puedes oler?

el pimiento & el polvo
lechuga & uva ahora
duros como músculos sus labios atraídos pa siempre
al vapor
se apresura desde
cafeteras expreso
familiares de estampados oscuros
"papi, está listo" como
algunas criaturas submarinas
de cuatro patas
elásticas de 6 millones
de años notorios
cholo agasao

cuando cita
a martí nadie se da cuenta
cepto yo por el
Malecón escondida en mareas que suben con
cada gimoteo de morena
grabado en nuestra piel
cómo podría conocer a
guillén la luz cubana
mañosa sobre
sus pies/ un buey
negro cubierto de cintas & medallas sangrientas
por su gracia asombrosa
cómo el son tropieza
sagrado desde su
risa & La Habana
vieja le frunce el

silk / his skin demands
a human touch
can you smell it?

the pimiento & dust
lettuce & uva now
hard as muscle his lips drawn permanently
gainst steam
rushin' from
dark patterned family
expresso pots
"papi, esta listo" como
some four legged
underwater creatures
lithe 6 million years
old a conspicuous
cholo agasao

when he quotes
Martí nobody notices
but me by the
Malecón hidden in tides risin with
each morena's wail
etched on our skin
how cd she know
guillén the tricky
cubano light on
his feet/ a black
ox covered with ribbons & bloody medals
for his amazin' grace
how el son trips
sacred from his
laughter & la Havana
vieja rolls her

ceño porque una vez
estas palabras *frágiles*
llenas de burbujas
de coney island
flotaron desde
la boca a la nariz
a Miami la negrita
torturada en santo domingo
cuya mami cosía
dobladillos de poliéster mientras
Trujillo imitaba
los sueños de Porfirio de su
propia estatua/
polvo de arroz suelto por el bronce de su ceja
mi lagarto estira
un miembro hacia
ramas de caoba
desgastadas por muchos
poetas cansados y solos

un búfalo de agua
que anhela una
cuerda de yomo toro
el lagarto al
otro lado de
la frontera cuyo aliento
se mezcla con el hibisco
dulce tequila &
mi cabello/ el lagarto cierra
los ojos/ su piel ahora
un crespón rugoso/
sus miembros amantes
de apaches galopantes
en las afueras de Denver/ a gusto
en baúles pintados

eyes cause once
these words *frágiles*
full of coney island
bubbles float from
mouth to nose
to Miami the tortured
negrita in santo domingo
whose mami sewed
polyester hems while
Trujillo imitated
Porfirio's dreams of his
own statue/
loose rice powder round the bronze of his brow
my lizard stretches
one limb toward
mahogany branches
worn away by many
poets tired and lonely

one water buffalo
yearning for one
chord from yomo toro
the lizard on the
other side of the
border whose breath
blends with hibiscus
sweet tequila &
my hair/ lizard closes
his eyes/ skin now
roughened crepe/
limbs cut-buddy
to gallopin apaches
outside Denver/ nestled by
painted trunks

de árboles grabados/ Q.E.P.D. (Que En Paz Descanse)
que dejan una gran fiesta
en Grand Concourse
o exequias en
Nueva Orleans/ nos
olemos desde
territorios separados

mi aroma me restringe
a suelos específicos
lejos de los
pantanos & ríos
el lagarto me atrapa por
los tobillos sin un
sonido el saco
tenso alrededor de
la boca de una caída
abierta/ "el cafecito
está dulce/ sí Papi"

cuando me contoneo lenta
en busca de mi estado
natural de reposo
mi piel es seda
pa tocarse
tatuada/ una iguana
de dogón en su
propia extensión
de huesos blandos/ pero no
en efecto/ mira/ estoy
acá/ no/ estoy aquí/
ves
crucé la frontera
justo debajo de tus narices

of carved trees/ R.I.P. (Rest In Peace)
that leave the Grand
Concourse a great
fiesta or New Orleans
funeral trails/ we
smell each other from
separate territories

my scent confines me
to specific soils
far from the
swamps & rivers
the lizard traps my
ankles without a
sound the pouch
taut round some
one's mouth fallen
open/ "the cafecito
is sweet/ si Papi"

when I wiggle slowly
seeking my natural
state of repose
my skin is silk
to touch
tattooed/ a dogon
iguana in her
own soft-boned
splay/ but not
actually/ see/ I'm
over/ there/ no/ I'm over here/
you see
I crossed the border
right under yr eyes

cinco

sus sueños se hicieron realidá & ocurrieron
lo hacen tós los sueños

            y ella era una cosita joven
no le quedaba ná   pa dormir/ un
mañana imaginado
que vino & se fue/

               el trompetista murió de sobredosis
               el bailarín era gay.
sus aretes
orbitan sus hombros
lo irregular era lo común

           soñó que una mujer era árbol
             asimétrico colgante
movimiento irregular en el almizcle de la noche
        (las mujeres & los océanos repiten simbólicamente/
          nunca de verdad)
& sus sueños ya pasaron
acabó las piezas
ocurrió el amor
aplausos vítores reverencias/ se aclamaron a sí mismos
tó se acabó
            y solo era una cosita joven
no le quedaba ná pa conjurar
gastó su magia en hazañas bobas
en cositas
un poema aquí & allá   un/ brazo
una mujer que emerge   & llegó la lana
reconocimiento académico & poder
del espíritu
los espíritus de otros
provocaron que quisiese traerles

five

her dreams came true & passed
all dreams do

         n she wuz jus a yng thing
wit nothin left   to sleep on/ a
tomorrow imagined
jus come & gone/

         the hornplayer o.d.'d
         the dancer waz gay.

her earrings
loopin her shoulders
irregular waz commonplace

        she dreamt a woman waz a tree
         asymmetrical danglin
uneven motion in the night musk
     (women & oceans repeat symbolically/ never in fact)

& her dreams had passed
the pieces were finished
love happened
applause cheers bows/ encored themselves
it waz all over

        n she wuz jus a yng thing
wit nothin left to conjure
her magic spent on small feats
lil things
a poem here & there   an/ arm
some woman burstin   & fleece spun
academic recognition & power
of the spirit
other people's spirits
made her wanna bring em

sueños/ muchos
quien quiera que quieras ser hazlo/ hazlo tú mismo
& roquea/ roquea/ rrrrrooooqqquueeaa
lo tuyo beibi

la amaron
porque liberó a alguien más de la oscuridad
les daba una rosa amarilla
tó por el sueño
& el de ella
ya pasó
muerto como cualquiera sabe
que albert ayler está muerto
the jazz lady está muerta & bessie...
su melodía viva se
mata en la avenida c/
no le queda ná   pa/ levantarse
                                      y bailar por ahí
las canciones estaban sincronizadas/ terminaron a la señal de un
    espíritu egoísta
que merodeaba en la lluvia
                es sufisiente/ es sufisiente
                los sueños son muy posibles
                muy posibles pa lo real/
                no quería otra cosa que la
                plenitud de su vientre
                en sus dedos
                fuera vida/ ceñida con plumas
                & plata
                enmascarada en colores de naranja & albaricoque
                soñó como una cosa salvaje
                & por un minuto
                solo un minuto
                sabría

dream/ s
whoever ya wanna be take it/ in yrself
& rock/ rock/ rrrrockkkk
yr own baby

she waz loved
cuz she freed somebody else from the dark
gave em a yellow rose
all for the dream
& hers
had passed
dead like anybody knows
albert ayler is dead
the lady is dead & bessie . . .
her livin melody killin
itself on avenue c/
nothin left   to/ get up
                           n dance abt
songs were timed/ ended on a cue from a selfish spirit
roamin in the rain
              that's enuf/ that's enuf
              dreams are too possible
              too possible for real/
              she didn't want but the
              fullness of her womb
              in her fingers
              to be life/ girded with feathers
              & silver
              masked in orange & apricot smells
              she dreamed like a wild thing
              & for a minute
              jus a minute
              she'd know

palabras/ piernas trigueñas música/ & ropa
ay & mentiras puños caos/ & trozos
de sueños/ pa envolverlos en trozos/
de sueños /pa acurrucarse
una criatura salvaje en peligros
de su propia autoría
(qué hará una trompeta por ti ahora/
cuánta coca puedes usar/ habrá
alguna foto tuya/ que no se haya convertido
en piedra)
ajááááááááááááááááááááááááááááááááá/

              soñar sueños
           desear deseos
       vivir una vida digna
    de reconocimiento

vivir sueños te volverá loca
vivir sueños te llevará al
final/ de ti misma
& sus sueños habían pasado
el independentista fue a la cárcel
el ceramista era impotente
    (sus poemas acumularon polvo/
     los públicos imploraban cómo los hacía/
       conocer otro lugar/ donde
ellos también/ podrían pasear sin miedo)
pero los gatos murieron
el periquito se fue volando
el carro se descompuso
un amigo la violó
enfamil era una palabra obscena
& pasaron los sueños
no le quedó más que dormir en las sobras
de otros tiempos/

———

words/ brown legs music/ & cloth
uh & lies fists chaos/ & shreds
of dreams/ to be wrapped in
shreds/ of dreams/ to cuddle herself
a wild creature in dangers
of her own makin
(what'll a horn do for ya now/
how much coke cd ya use/ is there
any photo of yrself/ that hasnt turned
to stone)
ahhaaaaaaaaaaaaaaaaaaaaaaaa/

dream dreams
wish wishes
live a life worth
reckonin

livin dreams'll make ya crazy
livin dreams'll lead ya to the
end/ s of yrself
& her dreams had passed
the independentista went to jail
the potter waz impotent
   (her poems gathered dust/
    audiences craved how she made em/
     know another place/ where
they too/ cd saunter unafraid)
but the cats died
the parakeet flew off
the car broke down
a friend raped her
enfamil waz a dirty word
& the dreams passed
she waz left to sleep on scraps
of other times/

———

solo había deseado cositas chiquitas
cajas de joyas & arco iris
hombres audaces con ternura & crueldá
como si ella
siempre viviera sus sueños
logrando que algo se haga ná más que una visión
& ella amaba estas cosas
las plantas el sillón
cualquier calle de san francisco cuando entraba la niebla
cómo el sol la levantaba cada mañana
se levantaba al calor
al que no hubiera cosa que no supiera
ni un sueño que no pudiera manejar
ni un atisbo de lo que tenía guardada pa sí misma
aprendió a soñar de forma muy íntima
pa que la relación continuara/
era ella lo que un sueño era

ná hecho algo
aliento & sangre una visión
un sueño vestido de crespón/ se fue por la ciudad
siguió con su vida como si hubiera intentado
no/ imaginar

sus sueños pasaron
como lo hacen tós los sueños
acumulados en los ojos

she had only wisht for lil things
               jeweled boxes & rainbows
               bold men wit tenderness & cruelty
like she waz
always livin dreams
makin somethin into nothin but a vision
& she loved these things
her plants the rockin-chair
any street in san francisco when the fog came in
how the sun picked her up each mornin
she woke in heat
to not a thing she knew
not a dream she cd maneuver
not a glimpse of what she had in store for herself
she had known dream too intimately
for the relationship to continue/
she waz whatta dream waz

nothin made into somethin
breath & blood become a vision
dream dressed up in crepe/ went out on the town
she went on in her life like she tried
not to/ imagine

her dreams had passed
as all dreams do
couched round her eyes

From *nappy edges*

páginas para una amiga

las cartas de amigos solían ser una forma de arte
observaciones literarias exquisitas pa el alma
estética y compulsión pa dar
orden a lo que sea que es esta vida
las páginas pa una amiga salvaron a muchas
pioneras / que subsistían junto al fuego en una casa de césped
del suicidio / algunas pioneras
se mataron como quiera
las cartas de sus amigos
trituradas entre sus puños / los mismos
puños que golpean paredes al intentar
almacenar la suficiente furia pa no morir
pa no quemar el caldero que oscila
sobre el fuego / el cucharón demasiado caliente pa manejar
la soledad que acecha
        el corral un comanche guerrero

las páginas pa una amiga aletean
en el viento / deseos de aliento perdidos
que mueren por que alguien emerja sobre el horizonte
alguien / venga a hablar / por favor hábleme / ahora
no tengo a quién escribir
estoy tan sola que no estoy segura si recuerdo
cómo es que se lee
es que me he memorizado todas las cartas
que mis amigas me enviaron
podría recitarle algunas
déjeme prepararle algo de café &
podríamos sentarnos & hablar
por favor, señor, solo hablemos
antes de que se me olvide cómo &
me convierta en silencio.

pages for a friend

letters from friends used to be an art form
literary exquisite observations of the soul
aesthetics and compulsions to give
order to whatever this life is
pages for a friend kept many a prairie
woman / lingering by her fire in a sod house
from committing suicide / some prairie
women killed themselves anyway
the letters from their friends
crushed in their fists / the same
fists that beat walls trying to
keep up enough anger not to die
not to burn the kettle swinging
over the fire / the ladle too hot to handle
loneliness stalking the
          farmyard a warring Comanche

pages for a friend fluttering off
in the wind / lost breaths wishes
dying for someone to loom over the horizon
anyone / come talk / please come talk to me / now
i've no one to write
i'm so lonely i'm not sure i remember
how it is you read
you see i've memorized all the letters
my woman friends sent me
i could recite some to you
let me make some coffee &
we could sit & talk
please, mister, let's just talk
before i forget how & become silence.

From *ridin' the moon in texas*

231

estas bendiciones

he bailado con nicolás guillén bajo el sol cubano
he preparado pierna de cordero halal pa c.l.r. james una tarde de
   brixton
compartí chile relleno con el gran romare bearden en tenth avenue
   luego
me pilló el apagón en sardi's cenando un filete porterhouse con
crema de espinaca mientras brooklyn se quemaba y richard long
   pontificaba.
tomé fotos de manuel puig y mamá bailando tango
anduve el museo de arte de detroit con richmond barthé
cené pollo asado y salsa roja con león damas cerca de dupont circle
tomé expreso con guillermo cabrera infante y miriam en el
   apartamento al oeste de londres
volé en el mismo avión que octavio paz & estaba puesta & trepá
a la altura de margaritas antes de ir a la zona rosa o la plaza santa
   cecilia
bailé como un *jitterbug* al sonido del repicador de max roach
entre tós los collages de bearden
y senté a mi hija en la falda de sun ra pa que tuviera la bendición
   del conductor cósmico negro.
recuerdo cómo el hombro de cecil taylor
sabía a champán y cocaína
cómo no podía entender que a john biggers le gustara el futbol
   americano.
todas estas bendiciones me llegaron como respirar, viste,
fácil y sin un plan,
pero el mundo era lírico entonces, el genio tan de color que se
   podía oler
como los lirios orientales que me trajo lester bowie
al knitting factory antes de que él & malachi favors tocaran.
vivo en la música conmigo,
& estas bendiciones.

these blessings

I danced with nicolás guillén under a cuban sun
prepared halal leg of lamb for c.l.r. james on a brixton afternoon
shared chile relleno with the romare bearden on tenth avenue then
was caught in the blackout at sardi's dining on porterhouse steak &
creamed spinach while brooklyn burned and richard long
    pontificated.
Took photos of manuel puig and mommy in a tango
strolled the detroit museum of art with richmond barthé
dined on red sauce baked chicken from léon damas near dupont
    circle
sipped espresso with guillermo cabrera infante and miriam in the
    west london flat
flew the same airplane as octavio paz & was high
margarita altitudes before I lit la zona rosa or plaza santa cecilia
I waltzed like a jitterbug to max roach's snare drum
admist all the bearden collages
and sat my daughter on sun ra's lap so she could get a blessing from
    the black
cosmic conductor.
I remember how cecil taylor's shoulder
tasted of champagne and cocaine
how john biggers liked football I couldn't begin to understand.
these blessings came like breathing, see,
easily and without plan,
but the world was lyrical then, the genius so colored you could
    smell it
like the star gazer lilies lester bowie brought me
at the knitting factory before he & malachi favors played.
I live in music with me,
these blessings.

una palabra es un milagro

una palabra es un milagro
solo letras que de alguna forma colman
a dedos torpes/ de significado
mi vida era inarticulada
nadie sabía lo que quería decir
no podía capturar belleza alguna o memorias tristes
una palabra en una página en blanco, sin embargo
eso es un triunfo
una ilusión infinita/ hecho acérrimo
de este reguero de mundo en el que
envenenan ciudades enteras y mi universo
es un error   una palabra
atrae yihadistas/ bendice a leprosos
urge revoluciones, una sonrisa.
un milagro de sonido
que hay que venerar

a word is a miracle

a word is a miracle
just letters that somehow wind up
clumsy fingers/ with meaning
my life was inarticulate
no one knew what I meant
I cd capture no beauty or wistful memory
a word on a blank page, though
that is triumphant
infinite illusion/ hard core fact
of this messy world where
whole cities are poisoned and my univese
is an error   a word
beckoning jihadis/ blessing lepers
urging revolutions, a smile.
a miracle of sound
to be cherished

un poema real

(para mi amigo, Chuka)

alguien me dijo una vez
que cada hombre no es un poema
pero algunos hombres son poemas de y por sí mismos
eucaliptos y lirios
atienden su llegada
besos ligeros
traicionan su ternura
a veces un abrazo es testigo
de densos secoyas y cipreses
que crecen por el pacífico
las peñas muestran su fuerza
granadas enteras
su delicadeza
qué hacer con un poema en dos patas
cuyo tacto trae temblores
a su alma un hombre sensible y
extraordinario en este mundo
*dame un momento solamente un momento**
en su presencia
soy bendecida
una mujer en el reino de un poema
sobre dos patas

---

* Cursiva en español en texto de partida.

an actual poem
(for my friend, Chuka)

some one once told me
every man is not a poem
but some men are poems in and of themselves
eucalyptus and lilies
harken their coming
slight kisses
betray their tenderness
sometimes a hug bears witness
to dense redwoods and cypress
growing by the pacific
boulders manifest their strength
whole pomegranates
their delicacy
what to do with a poem on two legs
whose touch brings quivers
a su alma un hombre sensible y
extraordinario en nuestro mundo
dame un momento solamente un momento
in his presence
and i am blessed
a woman in the realm of a poem
on two legs

oda a orlando

el pulso/ es común pa tós nosotros//
nos deja saber/ que podemos respirar
pero/ una noche/ solo había humo de cañón y llamas
la sangre /y pies danzantes detenidos
una noche/ mi hija que adora bailar /que es gay
quepodríahaber estado allí/ dehaber llevado a su hija
a un parque temático a jugar e/ imaginar
podríahaber/ trepao los cuerpos /sudorosos
sangrientos/ eran alegres ahora desparramaos bajolas
luces de la disco/ tan espeluznantes sonidos ahogados con gemidos
   & llamados al socorro
las banderas pasteles cubrían sus cuerpos/ durante el mes/ del
   orgullo
quizás/ una protección ficticia delas balas
esto está mal / en sus vidas así que tienen que morir.
estos jóvenes buscagozo en disfraces de escándalo &/ vigor
que podían ser/ un yihadista loco /un blanquito racista/ un hombre
   de negocios bien vestido
quienquiera que alimente la baba del odio y luego se sorprenda por
   los cuerpos que se esconden
en el baño /con el pistolero a la espera de la muerte/ esa pudohaber
   sido mi hija

eñangotá en la esquina/ intenta que no la vean
cuando tó /sobresu vida tenía que ser visto\su esposa\su amante\
   la mujer
a quien dedica el amor /eran abiertas & orgullosas
& visibles/ ahora manchás con hollín de pólvora y sangre

tanta sangre/ de tantos cuerpos
/ queahora buscan/ respirar
en /pulse/

ode to orlando

the pulse/ is common to all of us//
letting us know/ we can breathe
but/ one night/ there was only gunsmoke and flames
blood /and dancin feet made still
one night/ my daughter who loves to dance /who is gay
wda been there/ had she taken her daughter
to a theme park to play and/ imagine
she wda been/ climbin over the bodies /sweatin
bloody/ usedta be gleeful bodies now strewn neath the
disco lights/ so eerie sounds jammed with moans & pleas for help
during pride/ month the pastel flags coverin their bodies
maybe/ make believe protection from gunfire
it is wrong / their lives so they must die.
these young joy seekers in outrageous costume &/ vigor
that may be/ a jihadi freak /a white trash bigot/ a button down
    business man
whoever feeds the slime of hate and then is amazed at the beings
    hidin
in the bathroom /with the shooter waitin to die/ that cd have
    been my daughter

crouchin in the corner/ tryin not to be seen
when everything /abt her life was to be seen\her wife\her lover\
    the woman
she dedicated her love to /they were open & proud
& visible/ now smudged with soot gunpowder and blood

so much blood/ from so many bodies/
now seekin/ breath
at /the pulse/

es pa asegurarnos que tenemos //
mucha respiración acelerá /jadeos/ y/ quejidos
qué hacer ahora al arrastrarse sobre los cuerpos/ moviéndose/
	pedazos de huesos sangrientos/
fuera del camino/ un brazo\aquí\ un dedo separado de una mano &
cuellos/ apenas pegaos a sus cabezas/ medio destruidas
'acaso hay negros aquí/ notengo na contra' los negros
pero/ los mató/ porque andaban conlos gays
eran negros y gays/ como mi hija/ adolorida
de arrastrarse/ porentre las pilas de cuerpos sangrientos
acribillaos al ritmo/ de la música que disfrutaban
tanto que pensaban/ que los tiros eran/ el bajo
de la música/ que los hacía /sacudirse/ remenearse & retorcerse
al ritmo & los mataron rápido/ como los brazos
que cortan/ el aire/ al ritmo/ mientras caían de uno en uno
encima unos de otros/ sus últimos suspiros reflejan
el gozo de bailar/ bailan enla caradel terror/
a cámara lenta/ corrieron/ pa esconderse aonde sea
a guardar/ sus cuerpos gays/ en algún lugar seguro como
las losetas/blancas/del baño/liberados de la música
que tanto ansiaban/ahora callada/cepto por los sonidos
de la supervivencia//
		cuándo vendrá alguien a parar tó esto
toa esta sangría de órganos y tendones expuestos
& huesos que se asoman de la carne/   quién los salvará
vendrá alguien   a ayudar a mi hija/ atrapá en las
pilas de tejido sangrante & herido tan gay libre & gozoso
cuando llegaron quedaría alguien con pulso
49 de ellos no sobrevivieron   esta vez mi hija no estaba allí/

is to assure us we have //
so much heavy breathin /gasps/ and/ groans
what to do now crawlin over the bodies/ movin/ shards of bloody
    bones/
out of the way/ an arm\here \ a finger separated from a hand &
necks/ barely attached to heads /half blown away
'are any blacks in here/ I don't have anything' against blacks
yet/ he killed/ them cuz they were there with the gays
they were black and gay/ like my daughter/ achin
from draggin herself/ thru the heaps of bloody bodies
shot down in rhythm/ with the music they enjoyed
so much they thought/ the gunshots were the/ bass
of the music/ making them /writhe/ wiggle & shake
on the beat & they were shot quickly/ like their arms
cuttin/ thru the air/ on the beat/ as they fell one by one
on top of one another their/ last breaths reflectin the
joy of dancin/ dancin in the face of terror/
in slow motion/ they ran/ to hide anywhere
put/ their gay bodies/ someplace safe like the
bathroom white/tiled/free of the music
they craved/now silent/cept for the sounds
of surviving//
                    when wd somebody come to stop this
all this bleedin ripped sinews organs exposed
& bones peekin from flesh/   who wd save them
wd anybody   come to help my daughter/ trapped in the
heaps of flesh bleedin & hurt so gay free & joyous
when they came, wd anybody be left with a pulse
49 didn't make it   my daughter wasn't there this time

la bebé de mamá

duerme, duerme, negrita, que tu mama está en el campo, negrita
duerme, duerme, mabila, que tu mama está en el campo, mabila
duerme, duerme, negrita, que tu mama está en el campo, negrita
duerme, duerme, mabila, que tu mama está en el campo, mabila

queremos que sally walker
nos baile la pelusa
queremos que sally walker
nos baile la pelusa
pelusa por aquí
pelusa por atrás
pelusa por delante
pelusa por detrás

ahora te toca a ti

mama's little baby

mama's little baby likes shortnin, shortnin,
mama's little baby likes shortnin bread
mama's little baby likes shortnin, shortnin,
mama's little baby likes shortnin bread

little sally walker, sittin in a saucer
rise, sally, rise, wipe your weepin eyes
an put your hands on your hips
an let your backbone slip
o, shake it to the east
o, shake it to the west
shake it to the one
that you like the best

you're it

From *for colored girls who have considered suicide/ when the rainbow
is enuf*

chicago en sanfrancisco & tú/ yo/ esperaa/ el amor es músika/ tócame
como los sonidos/ chicago en mi hombro/ tu mano/ es ahora un beso
(para thulani & joseph)

me inspiro en medio dela noche
cuando me haces el amor

luego de haberte abrazao & besao & sentido tó eso -
me inspiro me quiero/ libre de dolor/
sin saber ya lo que es un sueño/ pero acaso es el amor como me
cantan odawalla/ *reese & the smooth ones*/ aquí donde me
besaste/ & te siento/ podría inventármela de nuevo/ pero ya somos
    músika
joseph roscoe lester don & malachi/ los oigo en nuestro sudor
& nadie habla/ pero los ritmos son melodía/ de chicago a la
fuga/ cuando me haces el amor/ grito como los colores que asume
    la cara
de joseph/ estoy atada al aire como el saxo de roscoe/ como si
    cartearan los 'naipes'
a nuestro favor/ una cosa con un toque de morena bip-bup-da-chi-
    dup-bliiiiiba-uh/ que refunde un falso romance/
    cuando noera loque querías/ o noera quien creías
que venía/ pero la ternura fue real/ no pue'e mentir
                              lo recuerdo
las cartas tienen que tener la baraja entera/ tengo que tener una
    mujer/ la reina de
espada/ como malachi entraba deslizándose con la gracia de
    nefertiti o eubie
blake/ esto noes loque esperábamos
                    EL ART ENSEMBLE OF CHICAGO
pero era de color/ era verdá/ era tener ritmo/ como te siento
a ti

chicago in sanfrancisco & you/ me/ waait/ love is musik/ touch me
like sounds/ chicago on my shoulder/ yr hand/ is now a kiss

(for thulani & joseph)

i get inspired in the middle of the nite
when you make love to me

after i've held you & kissed you & felt alla that
i get inspired get cherished/ free of pain/
not knowin anymore what is dream/ but is love like they are singin
to me odawalla/ reeese & the smooth ones/ here where you kissed
me/ & i feel you/ i cd make it up again/ but we're already musik
joseph roscoe lester don & malachi/ i hear em in our sweat
& nobody is speakin/ but the rhythms are chicago/ melody on the
loose/ when you make love to me/ i shout like the colors on
    joseph's
face/ am bound to air like roscoe's horn/ like the 'cards' are stacked
in our favor/ one slight brown thing bip-bloo-dah-shi-doop-
    bleeeeha-uh/ refusin false romance/
    when it waznt what ya wanted/ or who ya thot
was comin/ but it waz real tenderness/ cant lie
                    i remember
cards always gotta have a full deck/ gotta have a woman/ queen of
spades/ like malachi slipped in wit the grace of nefertiti or eubie
blake/ this aint what we expected
            THE ART ENSEMBLE OF CHICAGO
but it waz colored/ waz truth/ waz gotta rhythm/ like you feel to
me

tenía muchas ganas de ser mesera pa servirles como una negra/
    abrirme camino con
la cintura en una falda negra apretá & andar sin prisa como un alto
    en boca de bird/
un secreto/ demasiado dulce pa aguantar lágrimas/ quería músika/
    & me trajeron
amor en un millón de tonos/ & ya no soy la misma/ ya no
lo soy/ querías un suspiro/ hice como una flauta/ jalo/ me relajo &
fliii-ba-fla-fli-do-fle-do-fao/ suenan como caña nueva que no pue'e
    parar
'cherokee'/ 'a jackson in yr house'/ 'congliptis'/ por toas partes/
el art ensemble podría hacerte amar más/ podía hacerte amar más/

chocolaté o miz t. toda de plata/ no me inspiran como me ins-
piro cuando me abrazas en harmonías de chicago/ & valsamos
    como va-
gos/ levántate/ da la señal de liberar el dolor/ grita/ canta/ luego
    suspira/
gime/ suena/ haz el sonido que me besa/ una nota/ tú/ me haces
melodía/ es/ es la músika/ ay verdá ay/ sí/ la músika es lo menos
    que debe
traerte el amor/ lo más que tós ustedes jamás tendrán/ tú/ sí/
    músika/ tú/ dejaque el amor/
te haga músika/ me besas como el sonido/ nosotros/ dejamos que el
    amor/ sea músika/
míranos bailar/ & deja que la músika/ recíbela toda/ agarra la
    música/ deja
que la músika te ame/ cerca/ como el silencio

i really wanted to be a waitress to serve em in a negress way/ push
my waist thru a tight black skirt & amble like a alto in bird's mouth/
a secret/ too sweet to hold tears/ i wanted musik/ & they brought
love in a million tones/ & i am not the same anymore/ not any
more/ you wanted a sigh/ i made like a flute/ i pull/ i ease back &
splee-bah-wah-she-do-the-do-tso/ ring like a new reed cant stoppa
cherokee/ a jackson in yr house/ congliptis/ all round/
the art ensemble cd make ya love more/ cd make you love more/

chocolaté or miz t. in all her silver/ dont inspire me like i get in-
spired when you hold me in chicago harmonies/ & we waltz like va-
grants/ get up/ signal the release of pain/ scream/ sing/ then sigh/
groan/ sound/ make the sound that kisses me/ one note/ you/ make
me melody/ is/ is musik/ uh true uh/ yes/ musik is the least love
shd bring ya/ most ya'll ever have/ you/ yes/ musik/ you/ let love/
musik you/ you kiss me like the sound/ we/ let love/ is the musik/
watch us dance/ & let the musik/ you take it all/ get the musik/ let
the musik love you/ close/ like silence

From *nappy edges*

ACKNOWLEDGMENTS

This collection of my work would not have been possible without the help of my family and my very close friends. In 2004, I had a stroke and forgot how to read, how to use my mouth, and how to use my hands. It took years of physical rehabilitation and speech therapy along with the care of my daughter Savannah and my dear friend Claude Sloan. As I recovered I was able to write some poems for children's books and a poem for Pedro Pietri. Then, several years later, in 2011, July 29 at approximately 2:00 p.m. in the afternoon, I had my first episode of severe neuropathy, where I lost control of all my limbs and my extremities. I was wheelchair bound and unable to feed myself or walk. I had to use a trapeze bar to sit up. I couldn't hold a book or pay attention to people talking to me because my body was constantly trembling and demanding my attention. I could not write. Dragon 13, the speech-recognition computer program that allows you to dictate and have the words transcribed, did not work for me because the visceral feel of paper and pen or keys and fingers was inescapable.

There were no poems for six years.

One night a poem roamed around my head. I couldn't sleep or watch television. I tried to write it but the pencil hurt my fingers and my hands slipped off the iPad. The only thing left was the computer. But my fingers had not been strong enough to press the keys. I tried anyway. And a poem came out. This was my miracle.

And so, this collection exists, aided by the careful ear of my agent Rob McQuilkin and Lexi Wangler. Many thanks are due to my manager and friend, Donald Sutton of Global Artists Management, whose wisdom, persistence, and acute aesthetic taste has added order and vigor to my creative life. The new poems were all written within the last eighteen months. And the older ones, over the last thirty years. It is wonderful to see my work catch up to itself.

This would not have been possible without the friendship and support of Mickey Davidson, Flemmie Kittrell, Evette Lewis, Craig Harris and George Sams. I owe a great deal to my darling mother, Eloise Owens Williams, who cared for me after my stroke, and tended to me after my surgeries until she died. Without her I would not have made it. Above all, the belief in me of my sisters, Bisa Williams and Ifa Bayeza, and my brother, Paul T. Williams Jr., truly sustained me.

My aesthetic compatriots Thulani Davis, Miguel Algarín, Jessica Hagedorn, Dyane Harvey and Diane McIntyre, David Murray, Wopo Holup, Hammiett Bluiett, Felipe Flores, Woodie King, Luciana Polmey, Renée Charlow, and Michael Denneny kept my imagination alive and vivid. I want to thank Barnard College for salvaging the artifacts of my manuscripts and life. I want to thank President Barack Obama and First Lady Michelle Obama for their lovely note during the depths of my illness. I also thank all my doctors and therapists who have pushed me beyond my own perceived limitations. Finally, the love of my daughter, Savannah Shange, and my daughter-in-law, her partner Kenshata Watkins, and my new granddaughter, Harriet, have made my life worth living. To see this work come to life is astonishing and gratifying beyond my dreams. I am grateful to my professional organizations, the Dramatists Guild of America and P.E.N.

Lastly, I would like to thank my new editor, Dawn Davis, and her assistant, Lindsay Newton, for their care and assistance with this manuscript. It has been marvelous working with them. The delicacy and vivid imagery lent to my work by the poet and translator Alejandro Álvarez Nieves, Ph.D., and the poet Mariposa Fernández, for her assistance in translation and copyediting, is astonishing and gratifying beyond my dreams. With them, I truly believe, as in my "lizard poem," "i crossed the border / right under yr eyes."

I want to thank all of my readers and my audiences for leaving me such fabulous and rich memories for all of my creative life.

Ntozake Shange
Somewhere in the diaspora

CREDITS AND PERMISSIONS

"once there were quadroon balls," "toussaint," "lady in blue," "lady in blue II," "never mind sister," "lady in brown," "the stage goes to darkness," "lady in red," and "mama's little baby" originally appeared in *for colored girls who have considered suicide/ when the rainbow is enuf* © 1975, 1976, 1977, 2010 by Ntozake Shange.

"my father is a retired magician," "for all my dead & loved ones," "just as the del vikings stole my heart," "on becomin successful," "nappy edges (a cross country sojourn)," "expiriese girl wanted," "lotsa body & cultural heritage/," "i live in music," "latin night is monday," "hands & holding," "tropical dance," "lovin you is esctasy to me," "between a dancer & poet," "elegance in the extreme," "telephones & other false gods," "the old men," "fame on all fours," "five," and "chicago in sanfrancisco & you" originally appeared in *nappy edges* © 1978 by Ntozake Shange.

"we need a god who bleeds now," "take the A train," "mood indigo," "in the blueness," "about atlanta," and "new world coro" originally appeared in *a daughter's geography* © 1983 by Ntozake Shange.

"from okra to greens," "rise up fallen fighters," and "crooked woman" originally appeared in *from okra to greens* © 1984 by Ntozake Shange.

"tango," "dream of pairing," "18 march 1984," "box & pole," "new orleans nuptials," "wrapping the wind," "dressing our wounds in warm clothes," "who needs a heart," "walk, jump, fly," and "pages for a friend" originally appeared in *ridin' the moon in texas* © 1987 by Ntozake Shange.

"i heard eric dolphy in his eyes," "loosening strings or give me an 'A,' " "a third generation geechee myth for yr birthday," "irrepressibly bronze,

253

beautiful & mine," "if I go all the way without you where would I go?" "chastening with honey," and "crack annie" originally appeared in *the love space demands* © 1991 by Ntozake Shange.

"live oak," "a word is a miracle," and "ode to orlando" originally appeared in *Konch Magazine* © 2016 by Ntozake Shange.

ABOUT THE AUTHOR

ntozake shange is a renowned playwright, poet, and novelist. Her works include the Obie Award–winning *for colored girls who have considered suicide/ when the rainbow is enuf, nappy edges, ridin' the moon in texas, sassafrass, cypress & indigo, betsey brown, some sing, some cry* with Ifa Bayeza, *three pieces, lost in language and sound, the love space demands, liane,* and numerous children's books. She has been the recipient of a Guggenheim Foundation Fellowship, the Pushcart Prize, the Lila Wallace–Readers' Digest Writer's Prize, a National Endowment for the Arts grant, the New York Foundation for the Arts, the Elie Wiesel Award, and three Audelco awards. Ms. Shange also won an Obie Award for her adaptation of Bertolt Brecht's *Mother Courage and Her Children.* Ms. Shange's work has been nominated for a Grammy, a Tony, and an Emmy. She has taught at the Maryland Institute, College of Art, Prairie View A&M University, and the University of Florida, Gainesville. Ms. Shange has one daughter, Savannah Shange Watkins, and one granddaughter, Harriet. Ntozake Shange died in 2018.